Systems Theory
in Action

Applications to Individual,
Couples, and Family Therapy

Systems Theory in Action

Applications to Individual,
Couples, and Family Therapy

Shelly Smith-Acuña

WILEY

John Wiley & Sons, Inc.

Library of Congress Cataloging-in-Publication Data:
Smith-Acuña, Shelly.
    Systems theory in action: applications to individual, couples, and family therapy/Shelly Smith-Acuña.
        p.; cm.
    Includes bibliographical references and index.
    ISBN 978-0-470-47582-9 (pbk.); 978-0-470-91020-7 (ePDF); 978-0-470-91021-4 (eMobi); 978-0-470-91022-1 (ePub)
    1. Psychotherapy.   2. Family psychotherapy.   3. System theory.   I.   Title.
[DNLM: 1. Psychotherapy—methods. 2. Systems Theory. WM 420 S664s 2011]
    RC437.5.S65 2011
    616.89'14—dc22   2010018072

*To my dad, Warren Smith, for teaching me patience,
perseverance, and dedication*

Contents

Acknowledgments

I OWE A debt of gratitude to the many systems that supported the writing of this book. I am reminded of the concentric circle diagram that appears in Chapter 2, which outlines all the systems that are influential in the life of a child. In a similar fashion, there are many groups of people who have had a direct or indirect influence on this book.

First, my social circles have indulged me by giving me a pass on committee work and hosting events and have provided advice and encouragement. I would like to thank Pam Booth, Megan Fante, Suellen Howard, Cora Neslin, Julie Savoie, Amy Tabor, and Kerri Ziller for cheering me on and Richard Evans and Char Elliot for inspiration that often felt divine.

Professionally, I had the very good fortune of training with Bill Pinsof, Jay Lebow, Cheryl Rampage, Doug Breunlin, and Peter Reiner. The intellectually rich environment they provided continues to sustain me. Both in Chicago and in Denver, I have also had the privilege of working with clients in individual, couples, and family therapy, as well as supervising psychotherapy training. I am awed by what I have learned from my patients, and I am so grateful to be able to do this work. I need to thank my clinical consultation group, Tim Dea and Bonnie Messer, who hold this work with me. I count on their wisdom, compassion, and good humor.

Much of this book is directly related to my work at the Graduate School of Professional Psychology, an essential system in my professional development. My dean, Peter Buirski, has been a mentor who has provided excellent guidance in so many ways. He leads us in striving to be the best practitioners and scholars that we can be, and his encouragement has been invaluable. My friends Lavita Nadkarni and Jenny Cornish have supported every aspect of my professional life, including sharing their publisher with me. When we see that individuals always exist in the context of larger systems, I can't imagine doing my work outside the context of the support I receive from Peter, Lavita, and Jenny. I am so grateful to have the chance to work with Marquita Flemming at Wiley, who is responsive, interesting, and consistently reasonable.

There are other members of the GSPP faculty and staff who have directly supported this project, most notably Michael Karson, who is always willing to discuss systems issues with me and writes so well about clinical matters. He also provided lucid and entertaining feedback on this manuscript. Erik Sween's deep thinking and interesting ideas are consistently inspiring, and I want to thank him for reading the manuscript and offering helpful comments. Others in the GSPP community have supported the project in a wide variety of ways, but all have participated in systems work with me. I am grateful to work with Mark Aoyagi, Tom Barrett, Judy Farmer, Judy Fox, Kim Gorgens, Lynett Henderson-Metzger, Fernand Lubuguin, Hale Martin, Lee Massaro, John McNeill, Julie Meyer, Laura Meyer, Artur Poczwardowski, Samara Rasmussen, Lupe Samaniego, Jamie Shapiro, Janet Shriberg, Ragnar Storaasli, and Tracie Kruse.

I also need to thank all of the students who have taken my systems theory class, and whose intellectual curiosity keeps me on my toes. I am grateful to Courtney Hergenrother for reading and editing the manuscript, and to the many students who have read parts of the work. Gift Wahiwe has been an amazing resource in tracking down sources and being generally helpful. I am very fortunate that my students have shared their energy and enthusiasm on so many levels.

Finally, I make the point that systems theory isn't primarily about families, and yet my family is my primary source of support and motivation. I want to thank my German family for their interest, investment, and acceptance through the years. To my parents, Charlotte and Warren, and my siblings, Suzanne and Wesley, I could not have asked for a warmer, more loving, and more encouraging family life. I am so grateful for all the ways that I can count on you. And on to the inner circle, I am thankful to have found Tony, the love of my life, and to have Monica and Evan, truly the children of my dreams. You are my secure home base and my sanctuary. Thank you for everything!

Preface

MANY OF THE examples in this book come from the classroom, and I wrote the book with students in mind. I have been fortunate in teaching a Systems Theory in Psychology course for doctoral psychology students for 17 years. This course is required of all first-year students as a part of a year-long theory sequence. Unlike programs that teach systems theory as part of family psychology, our program utilizes systems theory as a foundational model for general mental health practice. Because I have struggled to find sources that use systems theory in this broad way, I began to explore the possibility of writing this book. As I mention in subsequent chapters, beyond the fascinating but dense early texts on applying systemic principles to social groups, there was little available outside the family therapy field. Further, most of the writing done in family therapy was linked to one of the early theorists. I realized that a general systems text could take a step back from these specific approaches and could supplement one of the overview family therapy textbooks.

Many of the other examples in this book come from my clinical practice, and I also wrote the book for practitioners. The art of psychotherapy is a vital, dynamic process that continually keeps me on my toes, and systems theory has been a worthy guide through the process. As my work evolves and improves, I return to basic systemic concepts for insight and clarity. I believe that sharing clinical stories is a meaningful and interesting endeavor that both provides intellectual satisfaction and enriches the work that we do. I hope that the book will allow clinicians to review basic concepts in a way that invites them to reflect on their experiences.

Most students in the mental health field are learning to be clinicians, and most clinicians are lifelong students, so my dual purposes in writing this book overlap considerably. I have tried to translate the technical language of general systems thinking into common, everyday language. As a translator, I endeavor to retain some of the original excitement of this comprehensive, far-reaching way of looking at human behavior. At the same time, I hope to capture the practical utility of observing human interactions through a systems lens. I have used many of the foundational texts from general systems theory, family therapy, and couples therapy, and I have also included some of my favorite references from the individual therapy literature. I have tried to weave together these background sources in a way that will present you with the key elements of each source and spark your curiosity to go deeper into each theory. Even without going back to the original sources, however, I hope that you will feel solidly grounded in the core components of systemic thinking.

CHAPTER 1

Introduction to Systems Thinking

I OFTEN BEGIN my course on Systems Theory with a game that has the following directions: "The name of this game gives the rules of the game. It's called Letters and Patterns, not Words and Concepts." I then give some of the following examples and ask the class to join in with their own examples.

It is puppies and kittens, not dogs and cats.
It is summer and fall, not spring and winter.
It is cotton and wool, not silk and nylon.
It is mommy and daddy, not grandma and grandpa.

Generally, at least a few of the students have played the game and chime in with their own examples:

It is beer, pizza, and cheese, but not wine, bread, and chocolate.
It is football and soccer, but not skating and snowboarding.

Then I shake it up a bit and give other types of examples: It is bedroom but not jockey; it is broom but not steak. And finally I will try to make it a bit easier:

It is running, but not run; it is hopping, but not hoping.

At times, a brave student ventures an incorrect guess ("It is swimming but not skiing"; actually, it is both!), but usually students who haven't figured out the game sit with puzzled expressions until I explain the rules. Seeing the words on the page may have helped you uncover the pattern, and most people have an "aha!" moment

1

when the pattern becomes clear to them. The game involves including words that have double letters and excluding words that do not have double letters.

This game is deceptively simple, and participating in the game provides an interesting glimpse into human cognition. While the directions clearly state that words and concepts are not important, students always say that they could not stop themselves from looking for organizing ideas within the list of words. I start the examples by including words that do have some kind of conceptual connection, and most people move right to that level of analysis. The game shows the strengths and the fallacies that come with the way that we organize information.

I also like to start my course with this game because the mental shift that most students experience provides a metaphor for the mental shift that I experienced in learning systems theory. Systems theory has given me comprehensive and far-reaching conceptual insights, and it has helped me correct many erroneous assumptions that are embedded in my thinking or that may be part of our current scientific tradition. While systems thinking has developed from Western scientific traditions, systemic concepts move beyond the type of linear analysis that focuses on isolating and reducing phenomena. This shift is both simple and profound.

As a psychologist, I came to study systems theory through a fairly typical path, by working with couples and families. I initially worked as an elementary school teacher, and in that capacity, I became skilled at applying behavioral theories for classroom management. While there were many elements of teaching that I enjoyed a great deal, I found myself frustrated that I didn't have the ability to help students with more difficult emotional or learning problems. At that point, I pursued graduate work in clinical psychology. I was especially drawn to psychodynamic theories, as they seemed to explain the problems of my former students in a unique and meaningful way, so I replaced my behavioral worldview with an object relations perspective. While I interned at a largely psychoanalytic institution, I was able to do specialty training in a family therapy clinic, and the "aha!" moment arrived for me. Rather than making me choose between behavioral or psychodynamic theories, systems theory offered a bridge between these perspectives and examined how they could work together.

In addition to providing a foundation for multiple theoretical perspectives, a systems approach provided an interesting shift in my clinical work. As I was learning systems theory, I vividly remember beginning to work with a couple on the brink of divorce. The case was perplexing to me in many ways. Both Maureen, 42, and Vincent, 44, were bright, well-educated, and likable people who performed well at work and were devoted to their three children. Neither reported infidelity, substance use, domestic violence, or other dramatic reasons for their marital difficulties. Instead, Maureen reported feeling lonely and unfulfilled in the marriage and was considering asking Vincent to move out of the house. Vincent was baffled by Maureen's discontent and blamed her friends, several of whom were recently divorced. As I explored the problem, I could see individual issues that appeared problematic. Vincent was the high-achieving son of immigrant parents, and his surface bravado seemed to cover deeper insecurities. Maureen seemed to have plunged headlong into the marriage after the death of her mother 20 years earlier, and I thought that this grief was resurfacing as her oldest child was leaving home. But these individual explanations weren't as helpful as I had hoped, and I knew I was missing something.

As I sat in the therapy room with Maureen and Vincent, I began to understand that I needed to examine the development of their relationship, in addition to knowing about them as individuals. In the popular series of *CSI* (*Crime Scene Investigation*) television shows, the camera often surveys the crime scene, sometimes zooming in to notice an important microscopic detail, and sometimes taking a wide-angle approach to examine a pattern at a distance. Invariably, the change in the camera angle and focus reveals important evidence that was easy to miss at first glance. Similar to the way that the *CSI* camera work shows what is beyond the scope of ordinary vision, the systems theory supervision I received gave me the experience of being able to "see" Maureen and Vincent's relationship. Suddenly, their marriage became a character in the room, and I understood that the neglect of their relationship had left it feeble and underdeveloped. While I could remain connected to Maureen and Vincent as individuals, I could simultaneously see the richness of the space between them. It was a revelation to understand that their relationship was also my client.

Of course, this revelation did not establish whether they were going to save the relationship or end the relationship. But the focus on their marriage as a system allowed us to explore the balance between their individual needs and the needs of the marriage. I could zoom in and see the important details that each of them felt had been neglected by the other and then zoom back and highlight the ways that these details related to the big picture of their relationship. As the conversation shifted, both were able to identify the ways that they had turned away from each other, giving attention to work and family without nurturing the marriage. Further, this realization allowed each to invest in the relationship in new and meaningful ways. Maureen included Vincent in family activities in ways that allowed him to feel valued for more than his earning capacity, and Vincent took the time to go to movies and plays with Maureen, something he had previously refused. As they increased their level of involvement, they became warmer and more affectionate, both remembering times early in their relationship when they felt more connected and beginning to dream about what they might enjoy together when their children left home.

I am somewhat embarrassed to say that I was surprised by the changes in Maureen and Vincent's relationship. Thinking about them as individuals, I believed that their marital distress signified something unresolved in each of them. I now know that one of the dangers of emphasizing the problems of an individual is that this emphasis can minimize the healing potential of relationships. A systems perspective showed me that I was missing something crucial in seeing them only as individuals, and the focus on the relationship brought it back to life. Although I have also worked with cases in which the relationship did not revive, I found that the ability to understand individuals in the context of their relationship and to work on relationships as well as on individuals has been invaluable to my clinical work.

The knowledge of systems theory has enriched my work with individuals as well as with couples and families, and it has been useful in a variety of other contexts as well. Colleagues who know that I utilize systems theory often describe themselves in situations like the one I experienced with Maureen and Vincent, feeling that they are missing something and knowing that systems theory could help. When they ask me for resources to brush up on systems theory, I have found myself in a bind. I can generally ask questions about the case and find specific applications of systems theory that will be helpful, but what is missing is a resource that really provides an overview of systemic concepts.

I have four options to offer in terms of systems references at this point, and none of them meets the needs of my colleagues. First, I can recommend one of the original sources in applying systems theory to psychology, and my favorite is the classic by Watzlawick, Bavelas, and Jackson, *Pragmatics of Human Communication* (Watzlawick, Bavelas, & Jackson, 1967). This book is a fascinating source for many basic systems concepts, and it grounds these concepts in mathematical and physical sciences in a sophisticated and elegant manner. Much of the language borrowed from the physical sciences is awkward, however, and can be difficult to translate into more standard psychological principles. I recommend the book to anyone who has the curiosity and wherewithal to move through it, but it doesn't fit the bill for most clinicians and students. A second option is one of the general systems books that are meant to be useful in a variety of human systems (Hanson, 1995; Laszlo, 1972; Weinberg, 2001). Although these books also review helpful concepts, their applicability to the practice of psychology is limited. A third option is one of the excellent family therapy textbooks on the market, which both review general systems concepts and detail applications from various family therapy traditions (Nichols, 2010; Nichols & Schwartz, 2001). These books do an excellent job of reviewing the history of family therapy and of highlighting its contemporary use, but clinicians who are not involved in family work find their relevance limited. Finally, there is an outstanding book about applying family systems concepts to work with individuals, which uses much of the information that one would find in a family therapy text as a backdrop for working with individuals (Wachtel & Wachtel, 1986). But what is missing in the current literature is a book that addresses the broad themes of systems theory in psychology that utilizes clear, readable language and clinical examples.

The lack of other systems references in psychology quickly triggers one of my pet peeves, the merger of systems theory and family therapy approaches. It is very common for a student to tell me, "I find systems theory very interesting, but I probably won't use it, since I don't want to work with families." Depending on the day, the poor student making this comment may get a long diatribe about the relevance of systems theory to all of psychology, not simply to families. In fairness, it is true that within psychology, much of the application of systems theory comes from the family therapy movement of the 1960s and 1970s, so the confusion is understandable. Yet I find this confusion unfortunate because it limits the use of these concepts and minimizes the relevance of the theory. The use of systems theory as synonymous with family therapy seems especially unnecessary, as systems theory has been applied in business and other disciplines (V. A. Anderson, 1997; Haines, 1998; Senge, 1990). I have come to rely on the basic concepts of systems theory as the foundation of my practice, and I believe that these core concepts have provided consistent, helpful grounding. As current discussions about the integration of psychological services into medical and educational systems have increased, I see that systems concepts could be used as a helpful foundation for many discussions. The timing seems right to revisit a basic knowledge of systems principles, and it is my hope that this book can provide this type of foundation for work with all types of systems.

WHAT IS SYSTEMS THEORY?

So just what is systems theory? Many of the concepts that we will explore in this book are already familiar and have been described through other philosophical and scientific traditions. In some ways, the term *systems theory* is a misnomer, as there isn't a single definition or tradition that would qualify as a distinct theory. Instead, *systems theory* can be defined as a set of unifying principles about the organization and functioning of systems. *Systems* are defined as meaningful wholes that are maintained by the interaction of their parts (Laszlo, 1972). Using this general definition, systems can include organisms, social groups, and even electronic entities. Most of the concepts that I will discuss can be traced to the work of Ludwig von Bertalanffy, a biologist who was born in Vienna in 1901 (Bertalanffy, 1968; Davidson, 1983). An excellent discussion of Bertalanffy's work can be found in a biography by one of his students, Mark Davidson, who convincingly captures the way that systems theory brought together the cutting-edge trends of the last century. As discussed in the next chapter, Bertalanffy was reacting to the scientific controversies of his time by trying to examine biological phenomena in a holistic, methodical manner. Bertalanffy's 1968 summary work was translated into English as *General System Theory*, yet as the systems theorist Ervin Laszlo (1972) points out, a more accurate translation would be *General Systems Teachings*. Rather than trying to create a new theory, Bertalanffy identified general principles that could be used in a variety of disciplines to move scientific inquiry forward. His hope was to create a type of metaperspective that could allow a common language in multiple areas of study.

In many ways, Bertalanffy's hopes have been realized, as systems principles have been incorporated into a range of scientific paradigms. Parallel to Bertalanffy's work in biology, work by the mathematician Norbert Wiener (1948) also explored systemic ideas, which provided the basis for artificial intelligence. Using the foundational ideas of Bertalanffy and Wiener, the movement to use systems theory to create interdisciplinary study began to grow and develop during and after World War II. This movement culminated in several national conferences and meetings, most notably the Macy's conferences, held between 1946 and 1953 (Heims, 1991). The roster of these conferences reads as a who's who in systems theory, starting with Norbert Wiener and including the neurophysiologist Warren McCulloch, the social psychologist Kurt Lewin, and the anthropologists Gregory Bateson and Margaret Mead. It is difficult to know exactly what happened at these conferences and how they influenced later scientific study, as there were no written records of the proceedings from the first several conferences. Seeing who attended, didn't attend, and left later conferences leaves much room for speculation about the process of sharing ideas at this level. What is clear, however, is that systems ideas are currently influential in business, sociology, anthropology, and mathematics (Davidson, 1983). The specific application of systems ideas is unique in each of these areas, yet the fundamental concepts are surprisingly similar. In each area, a systems approach adds an emphasis on seeing problems in context, looking at how interactions create and maintain problems, and examining the ways that patterns can remain constant or change.

As we will see in upcoming chapters, the major roots of systems theory within psychology come from three major areas (Nichols & Schwartz, 2001). First, Gregory Bateson began to study psychopathology from a systems perspective. In 1954, Bateson joined psychiatrist Don Jackson in Palo Alto, California, to study families with schizophrenic members. By 1959, they had created the Mental Research Institute and were joined by psychologists Paul Watzlawick and John Weakland, as well as by other family therapy pioneers, including Jay Haley and Virginia Satir. Second, in 1946, Murray Bowen began working with mothers and their schizophrenic children at the Menninger Clinic, and by the mid-1950s, he had expanded this work to include large family groups (Bowen, 1985). He continued working to apply systems concepts to understand the ways that the extended family influenced individual psychopathology, first at the National Institutes of Health and then at Georgetown University. A third area of systems work came in the 1950s, when Nathan Ackerman (1966) was expanding traditional psychodynamic definitions of relationship problems at the Family Mental Health Clinic in New York. All of these practitioners and researchers focused on different aspects of systems theory, but all were involved in the shift away from examining problems in an individual and linear manner to looking more at context and circular causality, which will be explored in subsequent chapters.

Many would argue that the glory days of family therapy occurred in the 1970s and early 1980s and that since then, the field has been disillusioned with the overall efficacy of family treatment. There was certainly an enormous amount of excitement around family therapy at this time, and many within the field felt that we had finally found the ultimate answer to psychological problems. The original idealism of the family therapy movement seems quaint today, as we understand more about the frequently intractable nature of human problems. We are now more aware of genetic and biological influences on human behavior, and we have a more realistic picture of the difficulty of overcoming challenges such as violence and trauma. While couple and family therapy has remained popular, we are much more aware of the complexities involved in providing this type of service. At the same time, many systems concepts have been integrated into other therapy models. Ideas of context, culture, and bidirectional influence are part of virtually all psychological theories now, although these approaches may not directly credit systems theory for these concepts. It is difficult for a psychologist to make it through a day without seeing references to one of the major systems concepts that we will discuss.

I hope the case for the utility of systems theory will pervade each chapter, as I highlight a central concept in the model and link the concept to a major theoretical application. I have positioned each concept in relation to other scientific ideas, and I hope that you will be challenged to think about theory in both a broad and specific manner. One of the key advantages of systems theory is that it allows a metaperspective, and as a scientist and scholar, I believe that questioning our big-picture assumptions is essential. One of my favorite books in graduate school, Thomas Kuhn's *The Structure of Scientific Revolutions* (1970), outlined the way that scientific knowledge grows, changes, and is discarded over time. He posited that science is guided by a dominant paradigm, which he called "normal science," and noted that scientific evidence tended to be accepted if it fit with current normal science and to be marginalized or ignored if it did not, at least until there were sufficient inconsistent data to push for a reorganization of theory. He called this reorganization a scientific revolution, and the process he describes is consistent with the type of discontinuous change we will discuss in later chapters. Reading Kuhn helped me remember that being a psychologist is part of an ever-emerging process, and I think that systems theory can be seen as the same type of evolving, dynamic base of knowledge.

SEVEN SYSTEMIC CONCEPTS

For purposes of introduction, here I'll emphasize very briefly the principles that will be covered in the book, as well as show the basic format I follow. Each chapter is designed to cover a single major concept in depth and then feature a psychotherapy method that provides an especially relevant utilization of that idea. Of course, each of the psychological theories that I discuss contains many, if not all, of the concepts I will cover, so there is something artificial about linking a theory to one single idea. Further, many of the psychotherapy approaches I reference come from the family therapy tradition, perhaps making it appear that I have fallen into the trap of equating systems theory with family therapy. But my hope is that by consistently moving between a general concept and a specific theoretical application, I can show both the relevance and the utility of the general concept for many types of systems. Similarly, I hope that a discussion of both theory and technique will bring the concepts to life. I have found that the systems ideas we discuss are both basic and profound and that the best way to really understand each idea at a deeper level is to apply each in a variety of ways. I will use the terms *client* and *patient* somewhat interchangeably, as each term has a history in the ideas we will discuss, and both terms have distinct advantages and disadvantages. Similarly, I will alternate the use of gender language throughout the book, unless I mean to refer to a specific gender. Finally, the case examples that I will use are composites of actual cases that I have seen in my practice, but all have been modified or disguised to protect an individual identity. I have used bits and pieces of real clinical stories, but none of the case examples refers to a single clinical case. My hope is that I have captured a psychological truth in the case material, but I am determined not to create a feeling that I have betrayed any material or spoken at anyone's expense.

Going back to view Vincent and Maureen's relationship through the seven concepts that I will cover in the book, we can see that even on a preliminary level, a systemic lens offers something beyond what is available in other psychological theories. Starting with the idea of context, we can first look at their relationship as a whole and then examine the way that the marriage is embedded in other relationships. Vincent and Maureen both value their children immensely, but being in the family context doesn't enrich their relationship at this point. Similar situations exist with Vincent's work and Maureen's friendship networks. At this point, these other contexts compete with the marriage rather than complementing it. They put more time and energy into other contexts and thus have more positive experiences in other contexts.

After seeing all the relationships in which Vincent and Maureen are grounded, and seeing the connections between these subsystems, we can move on to looking at the unique way that systems theory addresses causality. A more traditional approach to causality might look at the individual problems that Maureen and Vincent bring to the marriage. Using systemic ideas of causality, rather than blaming Vincent's narcissism or Maureen's depression for the problems in the marriage, we can look at the multiple factors that contribute to Vincent's self-involvement and to Maureen's passive withdrawal. Further, we can see the circular patterns through which all of these subsystems influence one another and create the unintended consequence of a distant unsatisfying marriage. This emphasis on circular and multiple causality is less blaming than a linear approach and also provides a broader perspective on intervention.

Systems theory helps us understand how and why this pattern resists change and also gives us ideas about how the pattern can be transformed. We can look at the ways that communication keeps the problem locked in place but could also create an avenue for change. Vincent feels relieved when Maureen turns to her friends for support, as he feels inadequate in addressing her sadness around their children leaving home. Maureen sees Vincent's reluctance to listen more fully and supportively as a sign of his selfishness and lack of caring, and she withdraws from connection with him. He then labels her withdrawal as a sign of depression or a midlife crisis, reinforcing his rationale for keeping his distance. We can see that this communication reinforces the pattern and that it establishes a structure within the system that isn't functional. Maureen feels closer to her friends and to her children than to her husband, suggesting problems with boundaries and proximity.

Looking at the development of the structure over time, we can see that family history and development also influence the current problems in the marriage. The distant, formal relationship between Vincent's parents and Maureen's loss of her mother as a young adult give them no vision of how to create a warm, satisfying relationship after the children leave home. We can imagine that early childhood patterns reinforce this difficulty even further, as Vincent's template in relationships is to gain approval through external success, while Maureen's involves taking care of those around her, without an awareness of her own desires. The intersection of history and development further suggests that these problems are likely to be even more meaningful and painful as the couple faces a relationship with each other without the distraction of children.

Finally, a systems perspective uses social constructivism to examine the cultural narratives that give their story meaning but limit the possibilities for change. When Maureen attends a friend's divorce party and sees the prevalence of relationships ending as children prepare to leave home, it is easier for her to tell herself that the time might be right for her to end her marriage. Both Vincent and Maureen expressed different variations on cultural beliefs around middle age. Vincent discounted Maureen's feelings of sadness by attributing them to a midlife crisis, while Maureen was pessimistic about Vincent's ability to change, saying that middle-aged men are stuck in their ways.

Weaving these themes together, I had before me a rich view of all that had created and maintained the problem, but I also could tap into a wealth of intervention strategies for addressing the problem. I was able to help Vincent and Maureen identify a shared vision for their relationship, which had been given short shrift as they attended to other parts of their lives. As would be predicted by systems theory, when the marriage improved, both Vincent and Maureen reported that they were happier as individuals and that their family life was more satisfying. Their communication improved in quality and quantity, which in turn increased their connection and altered the structure of their marriage and their family. In making these changes, I believe that they not only reworked their own family legacies but also passed along a new relational template to their children. The interplay between relational and individual change was rewarding to witness and gave me a chance to experiment with systems theory directly. I hope that as we move into exploring these themes in more depth, you will have a similar experience of intellectual growth and experiential empowerment. These lofty goals are certainly consistent with a theory that seeks to explain everything from atoms to the universe.

CHAPTER 2

Context

E VEN IF YOU have heard the story of the blind men and the elephant, it bears repeating. Most sources trace it back to India, and it shows up in Sufi, Buddhist, Jain, and Hindu traditions. Even coming from these different perspectives, the basics of the story are pretty consistent. A group of blind men are studying under a learned religious leader. They are instructed to go and observe as much as they can about an elephant. The seven blind men go in to observe the elephant, and then the teacher returns to quiz them. One of them says, "I know all about an elephant. An elephant is like a tree trunk; an elephant has a 40-inch diameter, it's sturdy, and it's strong." The next one says, "No, no, no, you are incorrect! An elephant is like a wall, it's broad, and it doesn't have that circumference. You're right that it is sturdy, but you've got the shape all wrong." Then the next student says, "I don't know how you could be so misguided. An elephant is like a rope, it's full of fibers and it's bristly." So of course, they all start arguing among themselves about the true nature of an elephant. The teacher listens for a while, then stops all of them in their tracks and makes one of my favorite statements: "You are all right and you are all wrong. You all describe the elephant, but none of you know the true nature of an elephant. An elephant is all of these things, but none of these things is an elephant."

MULTIPLE PERSPECTIVES

The story illustrates the systemic concept of context in a couple of different ways. On the most basic level, the story shows the fallacy in trying to understand the true nature of any type of phenomenon. Our perceptions will always be somewhat limited, and so certainly having a

13

narrower perspective is going to be problematic, and yet how do we have a perspective that is not narrow? The task of creating a sufficiently broad perspective often seems almost impossible. Part of what we learn from the story is that any understanding of reality is always limited by our own individual context, thus our understanding depends on the part of the elephant directly in front of us. In therapy, it is hard for me to forget this story, because so frequently, people in couples and families are similar to the blind men studying the elephant. It is not uncommon for me to hear an argument similar to the following:

> "You need to be more firm and disciplined with our kids. They walk all over you! How are they going to learn to take care of themselves when you do everything for them? You've got to tell them no, and make them follow through on their chores. It is our job to be sure that they are competent and responsible."
>
> "But you are always yelling and screaming, telling them what they are doing wrong. Family life is supposed to be warm and pleasant, not like boot camp. You are always ordering them around! I want them to feel content and good about themselves."

The irony of this argument is that it is highly likely that both parents are right. Like the blind men arguing about whether an elephant is a tree trunk or a rope, from a distance one can see that it doesn't make sense for parents to argue about whether children should develop responsibility or self-esteem, that it is almost certain that parents ultimately want children to have both. But systems theory also helps us understand the inevitability of multiple perspectives, in that each of us will base our understanding of any situation on our direct experience, which will be influenced by a number of contextual factors. In systems theory, this shift in perspective allows us to examine the difference between "either/or" and "both/and" kinds of thinking. When we engage in "both/and" thinking, the questions we ask begin to change. Instead of which perspective is correct, we can ask, "How do these two things relate to each other? What context does each person draw from in presenting a perspective? What is the possible overlap between perspectives, and how do they differ? When does this perspective fit best, and when does it fit least?" So with the arguing parents, we would want to know: "When does structure work well in this family, and when does support work well? How does the idea of order and responsibility relate to the idea of care and self esteem? How could these values begin to complement each other, rather than competing against each other?" Referring back to the elephant story, it is easy to see that to understand the nature of the elephant, the multiple observers are going to have to listen to each others' perspectives. The parallels to human relationships are profound: the recognition that to truly understand a problem in context, it is imperative to listen to the perspective of each person involved in the problem.

The notion of multiple perspectives is also foundational to the practice of psychotherapy. Being able to say to a client, "I think there is more than one way to look at this" is a fascinating part of our role as therapists. Often, patients become mired in their experience of their problems and can't take a step back to see alternatives. We are implicitly invited to examine the problem in the broader context of the client's life, in the context of our expertise as psychologists, and in the context of our own experience with the client. We are actually allowed to be the wise person in the story and to share our metaperspective on the patient's issues. The trick is, of course, that once we are asked to act as the wise person in the story, we sometimes start to believe that we can actually see and understand the whole elephant. It is one thing to be able to say, "Have you looked at that from a different vantage point? There's more than one way to look at your struggle; let's try another perspective," but from there it can be surprisingly easy to believe that we know our clients' reality better than they do. While I applaud the wish for big-picture thinking that is inherent in systems theory, the fact that each of our perspectives is limited by our own context is equally essential in the theory. As we will see in greater depth when we talk about culture and postmodernist approaches in Chapter 8, there is a complex balancing act involved in using the expertise gained from our theoretical knowledge while also empowering our clients to develop their own expertise—especially when they are more familiar with a different part of the elephant.

MEANINGFUL WHOLES

Not only does systems theory recognize multiple perspectives, there is a second concept tied to the idea of context in systems that is equally foundational. The other concept is *nonsummativity*, a term used to describe the phenomenon that the whole is greater than the sum of its parts (Watzlawick, Bavelas, & Jackson, 1967). This is another idea that is not new, as it is frequently traced to the Greek philosopher Aristotle (Hanson, 1995). Part of the notion of nonsummativity can be understood through our human tendency to organize phenomena into

Figure 2.1 Young girl/old woman perceptual shift

meaningful wholes. Looking back to Gestalt psychology early in the 20th century, we are reminded of Max Wertheimer's work on human perception (King & Wertheimer, 2005; Wertheimer, 1959). This work illustrated the way that our brains will fill in the necessary information so that an ambiguous picture will make sense. One exercise used repeatedly to demonstrate perceptual wholes starts with the picture in Figure 2.1 and asks people to state what they see. This figure is credited to W.E. Hill, who published it in the *Puck* humor magazine in 1915 (Weisstein, 2010). Generally, subjects see either a young woman (who is turned away from the observer, with a fairly strong chin and a necklace) or an old woman, with a large nose, looking down.

This type of exercise is fascinating because we can observe a process that is typically unconscious as we make sense of our world. Most people naturally perceive one image or the other, showing that we immediately organize the drawing into something coherent. This helps to explain why we get too attached to the idea that our part of the elephant is the whole—our perception has organized it this way. For many people, seeing the other version of the picture involves changing the interpretation given to various aspects of the drawing. These exercises show the ways that our perceptions can shift, sometimes suddenly, when the context around them shifts. When I have a student who has a hard time seeing one of the two images, I try to have them identify one piece of the drawing, knowing that then the context will shift around it and that the perspective will then become whole. If they are able to see the old woman, for example, I might focus on having them see her nose as the young woman's chin. Rather than simply focusing on the new whole (it is a young woman; don't you see her?), the ability to start with a key part of an object and then build a new whole seems central to our perception. This focus on other parts of the whole helps us to modify what we see as figure (in the foreground) and what we see as ground (in the background.) I find this shift in figure-ground perception similar to what happens in psychotherapy, as clients attend to the things that they find most significant and important. Looking at issues from multiple vantage points often allows a significant change in perspective, as the perception is organized into a new whole. Once the shift takes place, it can also be surprisingly difficult to return to the original perception.

A similar way of looking at nonsummativity is to examine the ways that groups of objects become whole entities. Laszlo (1972) makes the distinction between heaps and wholes, noting that a bowl of peanuts is a heap, but a peanut plant is a whole. Going back to our definition of a system, we see that a bowl of peanuts is not an organized entity that is maintained by the interaction of its parts, but clearly a peanut plant meets that definition. Deciding whether a group of people meets the definition of a system can be more difficult. As we examine the concept of non-summativity, it is easier to see the kinds of interactions and relationships that turn groups into a whole. We all know about that type of synergy that occurs in some groups, where a certain mixture of people creates a feeling or atmosphere that couldn't be predicted by knowing the individual members. Anyone who studies organizations and teams is also aware of the effect of getting just the right dynamic between players to maximize success. It doesn't mean that the individual parts aren't important, yet often what we seek in groups is the feeling of being part of something larger. Living in Chicago during the ascendance of Michael Jordan on the Bulls professional basketball team, I was fascinated to see the interplay between individual performance and group performance. Of course, any team would benefit from having a world-class player like Michael Jordan, yet initially his individual skills were not enough to guarantee success. Under Coach Phil Jackson, however, something on the team began to change. With leadership, time, and practice, somehow these individual teammates were able to function much of the time as a cohesive whole. As any basketball fan knows, the Chicago teams headed by Jackson ultimately won six world championships. In this instance, it was clear that the whole was greater than the sum of the parts.

While the concept of viewing a system holistically may seem perfectly logical on the surface, we need to remember that a great deal of Western science is based on exactly the opposite concept. To go back to one of the founders of systems thinking, Ludwig von Bertalanffy, we know that much of our experimental procedure is based on isolating phenomena from their environment in order to reduce variability. To put Bertalanffy's worldview in context, the practice of biology was dominated by two opposing forces at the time of his training (Bertalanffy, 1968; Davidson, 1983). The first perspective, materialism, posited that there were key materials, or building blocks, that made up all living matter. Within the materialist tradition, the most important thing a scientist could do was break down any living thing into its core elements. In contrast, the vitalists felt that there was a significant life force that drove biological processes and that a mechanistic view of biology would ignore the primary force. This view can be illustrated through looking at two perspectives toward evolutionary adaptation. Within the mechanistic view, random genetic mutations occur that may or may not be favorable in the environment, and the vitalistic view suggests a master plan with a purposeful, final cause.

The brilliance of Bertalanffy's approach was that it ultimately bridged these perspectives by offering a third way to look at biology. Rather than simply arguing whether the mechanistic or the vitalistic approach was actually true, Bertalanffy took a step back to examine the ways that these ideas relate to each other and to see what the ideas don't address. In doing so, he noted that one major problem with the mechanistic view is that it works better with closed systems than with open systems. In closed systems, phenomena can be isolated from their environments and then reduced to their component parts. In contrast, in open systems, organisms are constantly exchanging information with the environment and are both adapting and being acted upon. The open system view reminds us that living things are always part of larger systems and are simultaneously comprised of smaller, component systems. As scientists, our wish is to break down anything we are studying into its basic, essential parts so that we can understand it, and of course, that methodology has given us great scientific advances. Yet the beauty of Bertalanffy's observation about open systems is that he identified the limitations involved in seeing parts outside the context of the whole.

LIMITATIONS OF LINEAR VIEWS

Scientists today continue to struggle with the limitations of this linear approach. One of my favorite examples comes from Michael Pollan (2006, 2008), who writes about the ways that an increase in the study of nutrition has actually led to a greater number of diet-related ailments. We are all familiar with the reversals in diet recommendations over the past few decades, but Pollan sheds light on the flawed science that leads to these fallacies. Using a reductionistic premise, scientists work to break food down into its elemental chemical components and then use this knowledge of the basic chemical process to address some type of an ailment. This logic has been used to address problems of obesity, and the application of this logic has had some surprising results. If we know that fat has more calories per gram than carbohydrates or proteins, then it would be logical to reduce the fat in foods, thereby reducing the caloric content. It should benefit both the health of the public and the profitability of the food industry to develop and market low-fat foods. Yet the unintended consequence of this seemingly sound scientific approach was an increase in the national levels of obesity. As Pollan points out, we don't know why this approach didn't work, but there are ample examples to suggest that this linear, reductionistic approach to studying diet and nutrition is inherently flawed.

An open systems approach would address the problem of obesity differently. Rather than trying to isolate the high-calorie components of the American diet and replace them with lower calorie substitutes, an open systems approach would look at obesity more holistically, trying to examine the ways that the pieces fit together. The diet and exercise patterns of people struggling with obesity might be compared with those who don't struggle, not only to look for single contributing factors (high-fat diet) but also to look for patterns of difference. For example, an open systems approach might look at the interplay between type and amount of food eaten, timing and amount of exercise, and family patterns in weight stability and weight gain over time.

Of course, by making the picture bigger rather than smaller, many of these questions can become overwhelming. While it is logical from a both/and perspective to say that heredity, number of calories consumed, freshness of foods eaten, culture of origin, daily duration of exercise, and daily intensity of exercise all interact to determine one's actual weight, this picture neither tells us what other variables we might be omitting nor tells us where to start in addressing the problem. Do we need to modify our patients' DNA, put them on a walking schedule, or stop them from eating processed foods to help them lose weight?

CONTEXTUAL CONNECTIONS

The good news about applying a systems perspective to problems is that there are so many ways to put the problem in context. It reminds me of our new ability to find places on Google Earth: The program starts with a view of an entire hemisphere and then moves to smaller and smaller increments to end with a picture of a specific residence. Going through Google Earth provides a graphic, almost visceral experience of the parts/wholes nature of systems theory, as you can see that your neighborhood is part of your town, your street is part of your neighborhood, and your residence is part of your street. Such a perspective evokes the work of Uri Bronfenbrenner (1979), a developmental psychologist whose model was known as the ecological systems theory.

The model, depicted in Figure 2.2, shows that an individual child is embedded in a variety of environments at all times and that it would be a mistake to try to understand the individual without taking these contextual variables into account. In this application of the model, each context has a different level of influence on the particular issues that bring the system to treatment. While not all variables are addressed in treatment, the ability to look at all of these levels provides a richer, more realistic view of the factors that maintain the problem.

Using this contextual model, we can look at the case of Ryan, age 16, whose parents came to see me in therapy. Ryan had recently been diagnosed with a learning disorder, and the psychologist who tested Ryan referred his parents to me for couples therapy. Ryan's academic performance was slightly below average, but he was doing fine socially, performing well in sports, and holding a leadership position in student government. He had a good relationship with his sister, Erin, age 13, whose academic performance was at the top of her class and who was also performing well in her extracurricular activities. His recent diagnosis helped explain why his academic performance wasn't better, an issue that caused long-term conflict between his parents.

This couple was Lisa, 44, a litigator for a large local law firm, and Bill, 43, who practiced real estate law for a small firm. Lisa was from the East Coast and grew up in a large, working-class, Irish Catholic family. Lisa attended private schools on scholarship throughout her academic career. She has received medication for struggles with depression

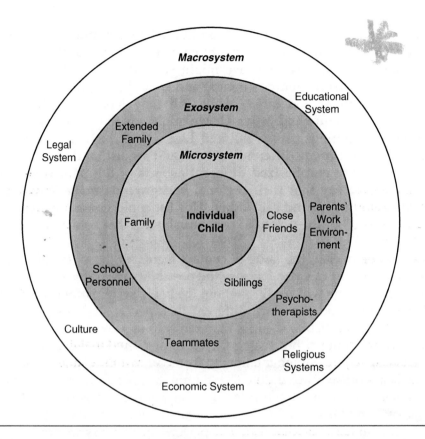

Figure 2.2 Adaption of Bronfenbrenner's Ecological Model Applied to a Family System. Bronfenbrenner, 1979.

and anxiety at various points of her adult life. Bill grew up in a small town in Wyoming. His father was the president of the local bank, while his mother was involved in many charitable organizations, some affiliated with their Protestant church. Bill received a number of tutoring services throughout his schooling, and now that Ryan has been diagnosed with a learning disorder, Bill believes that he has an undiagnosed learning disability based on their similar academic records. Lisa describes herself as driven and hardworking, and she strives to pass along a strong work ethic to her children. Bill feels that his success has come from his interpersonal skills, and he values being warm and friendly. Lisa feels that Bill does not provide Ryan with enough structure and needs to hold him more accountable for academic progress, while Bill wants Lisa to be more encouraging and supportive to Ryan.

As we go through each piece of additional information, you can see that each contextual variable might change the focus of the therapy in some way. For example, we might say that Bill and Lisa were born with different temperaments, and that she is programmed to be more vigilant and strict, while Bill may have a harder time providing structure and order. Or we might say that working in different legal settings causes Bill and Lisa to look at their household structure and climate differently. One could argue that their religious traditions have emphasized different aspects of the parenting role, or one could say that their regional backgrounds make it difficult for them to understand each other. This list could go on, as we move to examine all of the potential contextual parts that contribute to the whole problem.

For the clinician, the issue of context increases the possibilities for intervention but can also increase the possibility of confusion and lack of clarity. As you will see throughout the book, systems concepts work best together and there are different therapeutic strategies that are aligned with particular theories than can help us select the most salient elements of context. But seeing the client or client system as an open system, as well as taking the time to focus on various elements of context, is a worthwhile antidote to the limitations caused by our biases. Taking this idea one step further, we also see that psychotherapy itself is a contextual process. I especially enjoy the work of Michael Karson (2008), who uses his knowledge of performance theory to explore the ways that clinicians use their role to either maximize or limit their effectiveness in the room. Applying a systemic lens, Karson notes that dyadic therapy is in essence a couples therapy experience, as the context of the interaction is created by what both parties bring to the relationship. An open systems view highlights the fact that both client and therapist are changed by their work together.

SEEING PROBLEMS IN CONTEXT

One therapy approach that is practically synonymous with context is Murray Bowen's (Bowen, 1985; Nichols & Schwartz, 2001). While Bowen's approach certainly rests heavily on an understanding of family dynamics, it is one of the family therapy approaches that is most frequently practiced with individuals. Further, Bowen modeled an open systems perspective through his candid discussion of work that he did with his own family. For Bowen, one of the key elements of understanding the human psyche was to look at the interplay between the individual and the group. His theory provides a foundational view of the relationship between parts and wholes, as he focused on the ways that individuals simultaneously strive for autonomy and intimacy. According to Bowen, systems work best when they explicitly value the needs of both the group and the individual and when they have group norms that allow communication about these needs. Bowen's work exemplifies the use of multiple perspectives and shows the ways that functional families are open systems.

Bowen, born in 1913, was an analytically trained psychiatrist who became intrigued with the ways that family dynamics contribute to individual psychopathology. As mentioned in the previous chapter, Bowen did research on schizophrenia for the National Institute of Mental Health between 1954 and 1959 (Nichols, 2010) and had the opportunity to observe patients interacting with their families. While the prevailing notions of the time indicated that schizophrenia developed through the early interactions with the mother, Bowen was intrigued by the ways that current interactions might keep symptomatic behavior alive. Bowen also expanded the focus beyond the mother to include the entire family, and rather than looking only at early childhood experiences, he looked at the unconscious processes that continue to exist between family members at any given time.

Bowen is one of the family therapists known for developing the genogram (Bowen, 1985; Kerr & Bowen, 1988), a tool to diagram family membership and relationships, with shapes and lines representing each member of the system and their relationship to others. A sample genogram of Ryan's family is presented in Figure 2.3.

In this visual representation of the family context, Bowen stated that to truly understand a person's struggles, it was essential to see the problems in the context of at least three generations. Bowen borrowed from his psychodynamic roots by emphasizing the importance of unconscious processes that bind families together. He highlighted the patterns of shared beliefs and anxieties by exploring the family genogram.

BELONGING AND IDENTITY, THINKING AND FEELING

One of Bowen's key concepts is that of *differentiation* (Bowen, 1985), a term that he uses in two different ways. Bowen stated that individuals who are differentiated have the ability to experience both closeness and individuality and to utilize both thoughts and emotions in processing their experience. Both ideas have interesting ramifications for how

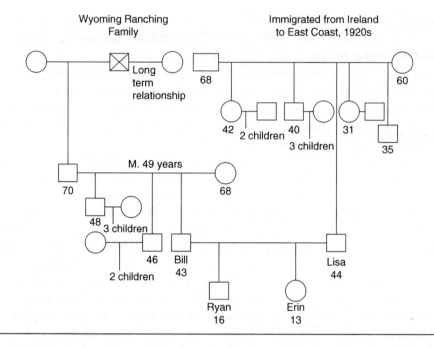

Figure 2.3 Bill and Lisa's Three-Generational Genogram.

people behave in the context of relationships. Through the concept of differentiation, Bowen provided an interesting perspective on the dynamic tension between the human needs for autonomy and intimacy. Bowen described someone as being differentiated if the individual had an established, separate identity and simultaneously had intimate connections with others. While the term *differentiation* may be confused with the concept *separation*, Bowen was clear that these ideas were different. More recent advocates of Bowen's theory, in particular, note that the idea of differentiation is a powerful antidote to the overly individual focus of Western psychology, as the concept promotes a balance between the needs of the individual and the needs of the group. More specifically, for Bowen, a healthy system will promote differentiation by providing opportunities for closeness and connection and also by valuing the unique identities of each group member. Sometimes these values can be expressed simultaneously, while at other times they are expressed sequentially, but obviously there are times when these values result in conflict.

Many schools of thought highlight the inherent tension between autonomy and intimacy, yet Bowen's concept of differentiation does an especially nice job of providing a big-picture view of this struggle. Bowen notes that some relationships may appear to be overly close, or fused, because there is no room for the needs of the individual. At the other extreme are relationships that are estranged or cut off, but Bowen points out that both patterns represent a lack of differentiation.

I find the concept of differentiation so helpful because in therapy, it is common to hear one of the two following comments:

> "I've resolved my issues with my family. I know this because I finally stopped speaking to them."
> "I don't have issues with my family. We talk all the time, and we never have disagreements."

Bowen's concept of differentiation not only shows the flaws in the logic of each of these statements but also emphasizes the way that each of these strategies addresses the same underlying dynamic. As we would expect in the both/and nature of systems theory, autonomy and intimacy work best as complementary concepts. The more a person feels grounded and accepted in a secure relationship, the more she will be able to express and be true to her identity. Similarly, the more a person has developed a distinct and congruent identity, the more he will be able to experience authentic intimacy.

Bowen also used the term *differentiation* to describe the ability to separate thoughts and feelings and to use thoughts and feelings together in a constructive manner. At times Bowen's approach is judged to be overly cerebral, with too much emphasis on moving away from reactive emotion, but a careful reading of the theory highlights the need for both affect and cognition. Similar to the need for individuals to be distinct yet connected, Bowen believed that problems were exacerbated when individuals could not distinguish between thoughts and feelings. Without this distinction, we are prone either to react impulsively based on our feeling state or to intellectualize problems and become overly rational. A more differentiated perspective allows us to think through problems and employ the benefit of our reasoning abilities, while also tuning in to our feelings and using the wisdom of our emotional reactions.

While Bowen advocated clear and direct communication to facilitate differentiation in systems, he also pointed out our tendency to avoid direct communication through triangulation. While many systems approaches discuss the importance of triangulation, Bowen outlined the development and maintenance of problematic triangles in helpful detail. According to Bowen, one way for two people to address the inherent anxiety associated with conflict between them is by "triangulating in" a third person. If we think about human nature, we can see that one reliable way of creating a connection with another person is to do it at another's expense. There is ample evidence in the social psychology literature, as well as from history in general, to know that one way to create cohesion within a group is to set the group in competition with another group—to develop a common enemy—but Bowen goes further in helping us understand that phenomenon of the common enemy in more depth and highlights the difficulty in changing this type of dynamic. According to Bowen, when some kind of conflict exists between two people, this conflict will naturally raise some type of anxiety. In relationships between individuals who are differentiated, this anxiety can be tolerated because it can be both felt and understood. In addition, because both parties agree that they will respect the needs of the individual and the needs of the relationship, it will ultimately be safe to address the conflict directly.

Without differentiation, however, the conflict becomes more dangerous because it threatens either the loss of self or the loss of relationship. So instead of addressing the conflict directly, it is easier to find a sense of pseudo closeness by bringing someone else into the conflict. The anxiety of the original conflict is then reduced because there is a sense of fusion with the like-minded person and a sense of cutoff from the conflictual partner, and the system once again rests in a steady state. To complicate matters further, Bowen says that systems that use triangulation to manage anxiety are prone to many levels of shifting triangles. Within these systems, we have the experience of shifting coalitions, which temporarily reduces anxiety but never truly resolves the underlying anxiety or the conflict.

REWORKING THE LEGACY

We can return to the case of Bill and Lisa to look at how Bowen would use contextual elements to understand and intervene in their conflict. As you can see from the genogram, Bill and Lisa have been married for 18 years and have two children, Ryan, 16, and Erin, 13. Bill is the youngest of three children and the only one of them to have moved away from the small town in Wyoming where he was raised. His great-grandparents came out West to homestead a ranching property, and Bill's family is well known and respected in the area. Both of his siblings are professionals who continue the family tradition of community involvement. There was a scandal in the family when Bill was a teenager, as after his grandfather died, it became clear that the grandfather had had a mistress for many years. This woman was well provided for in the grandfather's will and was persuaded by the family to sell her share of the assets and move away. The family has not discussed this issue since it occurred. Bill's family tends to be polite, cordial, and emotionally inexpressive.

Lisa is the oldest of five children. Her grandparents on both sides immigrated to the United States from Ireland in the early 1920s. Her father drove a city bus, and her mother worked part-time as a hairdresser. Her siblings now live in different parts of the country and have varying levels of professional success. One of her sisters and one of her brothers graduated from law school, and both have successful corporate practices. Her youngest sister is a social worker. A second brother has had significant problems with substance abuse and is currently living with her parents. Lisa's parents frequently contact her for legal advice regarding her younger brother's issues. He has been in and out of treatment programs and has experienced various legal problems while actively using substances. He was accused of stealing from one of his employers and also received a DUI. These events often lead to emotional scenes in the family, either in person or on the phone. At these times, Lisa is called in to strategize about fixing whatever problem her brother has created, and to calm the emotional upheaval in the family. Consequently, Lisa has mixed feelings about the family's inability to handle these problems without her help.

Referring to Bill and Lisa's genogram, we see the counterpoint of family resilience and family challenge. It can be easy to focus only on the problems in the family, and yet Bowen's approach encourages us to look at our ability to gain strength from reworking family relationships. In this case, Bill and Lisa are stuck in chronic relational conflict over their different parenting styles, which have become more polarized as their children enter adolescence. By focusing on the family context, we can see that at least some of their contrasting styles can be understood from the conscious and unconscious beliefs and values of each family. When Lisa wants order, structure, and productivity, she is expressing the values that have helped her move forward and achieve success. At the same time, Bill values cordial relationships and keeping the peace. He wants relationships to feel harmonious and supportive.

To start with a both/and approach, we can understand why each of these positions is valid and compelling for Lisa and Bill, but Bowen's approach goes a step further in helping us discern why it is so difficult for Lisa and Bill to use these perspectives together. On a conceptual level, we see unresolved issues in each family that make it hard for Lisa and Bill to differentiate. While their styles are different, their respective families exhibit an inability to deal with and move through the primitive anxiety that is generated by family problems or by family change. Bill's family dealt with his grandfather's secret relationship by getting the problem out of sight and detaching emotionally. Bill's family seeks harmony and positive appearance to the point that negative feelings are not acknowledged or addressed. This pattern is seen not only with his grandfather's hidden relationship but also in his parents' reaction to his learning problems. While he experienced a great deal of frustration in school and sensed that his parents were disappointed by his lack of academic achievement, these feelings were never discussed. The rational approach to the problem was to find tutors for Bill and to change the subject if it was raised.

Lisa's family moves in the opposite direction, engaging in loud and intense emotional battles when a family problem arises. There is a great deal of conversation and contact between family members, but like Bill's family, the patterns that exist between family members change very little over time. On a more practical level, the lack of differentiation is evident in the ways that each family participates in triangles. As Lisa becomes anxious about her son's uneven academic performance, she becomes angry with Bill's softer style, and the conflict between them increases. When Lisa talks to her mother at these times, they tend to commiserate about the ways that men are not helpful in raising children. Lisa's mother cautions her not to rely too much on Bill, because his family allowed him to be an underachiever and to fall back on the family business for his career success. Her mother often ends these conversations with negative comments about Lisa's brother, cautioning her not to let Ryan grow up to be like his Uncle John, which completes another act of triangulation. During these times of conflict, Bill is not likely to confide in his family. Instead, if an extended family gathering is imminent, he is likely to honor the needs of his family of origin over his current family. As a result, Lisa responds in an angry, emotional way, and Bill's family responds with perplexed, distant politeness.

A recent event served as a microcosm for all of these interactions. Lisa and Bill were driving to see Bill's family and celebrate his father's 70th birthday. As the plans were being made, it became clear that Ryan was going to have to miss one of his SAT preparation classes to leave in time to attend the first family dinner. Lisa wanted Bill to tell his family that they would miss the Friday dinner and would join the events on Saturday, highlighting the importance of Ryan preparing for college and following through with his commitments. When Bill stated that Ryan has already done adequate preparation, Lisa became angry and was quite negative about Ryan's academic skills. She called her mother, who reinforced Lisa's view that Bill was too easy on the children. In the meantime, Ryan stormed out of the house after yelling at his mother for being so critical and unsupportive. In the end, Lisa backed down and the family went to the Friday night gathering. As expected, Bill was cordial and positive toward his family, showing no sign of the stress that preceded the event, while Lisa was on edge and subtly rude. The interactions once again confirm the family pattern: Lisa is emotional and angry and makes her point but ultimately doesn't feel effective. Bill absorbs Lisa's anger but doesn't really work with her and ends up glossing over the problem rather than addressing it directly.

So what would Bowen do with this couple? If we are thinking systemically, it is clear that a change in the individual will affect the system and that a change in the system will affect the individual. In this instance, the couple has presented for therapy, so the emphasis will be on improving the couple relationship by helping each member of the couple become more differentiated. The first step in the process is to share the genogram with the couple and get their reactions. While this might seem like a preliminary step, it tends to be a powerful intervention in its own right. One of the goals of doing the genogram is to put the problem in a broader context. Using this couple as an example, Bill believes the problem is Lisa's negativity and rigidity, while Lisa believes that the problem is Bill's avoidance and lack of responsibility. Rather than defining the problems as behaviors, the couple starts the process by defining the problem as the other person. Yet doing the genogram allows the couple to see that the behavior makes sense in the context of family dynamics. In addition, the genogram allows the couple to redefine the problem: They can see directly that the problem is that they don't know how to work together for the benefit of their children, instead choosing to repeat the legacies of unproductive conflict and avoidance. They can see that several family patterns are going to make it challenging for them to work together but will ultimately make this change possible. So while it might appear that doing the genogram is simply creating a visual representation of the family, the process of completing the genogram necessitates reflection and curiosity and generates insight.

CREATING CLEARER CONNECTIONS

Following the explanation of the genogram, the therapist would help the couple discuss practical ways to increase their differentiation. If we remember the basic definitions of differentiation, we can see that this couple will have ample opportunities to practice greater differentiation with each other, as well as with their families of origin. When Lisa is worried about their son Ryan's grades and test scores, she can learn to feel the anxiety and talk with Bill about her fear as well as her anger. In addition, she can try to better integrate her thoughts and feelings by using information and affect together. Rather than simply assuming that Bill is trying to undermine her attempts to support Ryan's SAT preparation, she could ask Bill to help her find out exactly what Ryan will miss in Friday afternoon's prep session, and they could see if there is a way for him to make up what he would miss.

You are probably already thinking that Bill could participate in a similar endeavor, albeit for different reasons. Rather than passively trying to go around Lisa's wishes, he could be more active in expressing what he wants. Knowing that attending all of the family gatherings is important to him and to his family, he could look at the schedule ahead of time and make his wishes known to Lisa directly. You can also see that each action will be easier if both partners are involved in a different way with their own families. If Lisa were to call her mother to ask for advice rather than to complain about Bill and look for support for her own position, she might then approach Bill from an entirely different perspective. We can see that the act of differentiating feeling from thought, and learning to use them together rather than in opposition, is significantly easier when the triangulation isn't in place. When Lisa calls her mother to complain about Bill, the implicit agenda is to feel anger and rejection for his position and to be justified in this anger.

Bill's task is the mirror image of Lisa's. As Bill is more differentiated from his family of origin, he will be able to ask questions and risk conflict rather than keep the peace and focus on appearances. In this instance, Bill does not even consider calling his sister, who organized the Friday night party, and go over the possibility of missing the Friday event. Again, looking at unconscious anxiety in families, Bill feels that this kind of conversation just "isn't done" in his family. Without being able to articulate his discomfort, he knows that to mention that the needs of his nuclear family may conflict with the desires of the larger group is to threaten some kind of unspoken rule.

A hallmark of Bowen's technique is to use letters to facilitate differentiation. Bowen thought that letters were particularly useful because they were likely to minimize the expression of reactive affect. Bowen was also known for working with individuals by having them invite various family members into the session to facilitate differentiation. Regardless of the specific technique, Bowen would always advocate negotiation between the needs of the individual and the needs of the group, as well as an ability to use thoughts and feelings. Throughout the work, making room for multiple perspectives is essential.

As I worked with Lisa and Bill, it was interesting to see the ways that their work with their families and their work with each other dovetailed. As Lisa was able to moderate her fear of chaos and failure with a realistic view of her accomplishments and with the strengths of Bill and Ryan, she became less reactive and more able to express her concerns in a way that they could be heard. When less of the time spent with her mother and sisters was devoted to scapegoating another family member (usually John or Bill), she began to recognize how much her self-esteem was drawn from contrasting her achievements with their limitations. This insight allowed us to focus more on her genuine strengths, and she was able to identify the ways that she longed for connection with her family around their appreciation of her. As she was warmer and softer with her family members, she also became more able to share these qualities with Bill.

At the same time, Bill was motivated to gather his courage to be more direct with Lisa and with his larger family. As he was able to identify and share the ways that Lisa's criticism had hurt him, it didn't take long for him to get in touch with the loneliness and disappointment that he felt around his family's distance. While they were not overtly critical, he frequently felt emotionally unsupported, and instead of shrugging these feelings off, he began to look for ways to address these feelings with them. At times it was easiest to do this around Ryan's needs, as he was very aware of trying to be more emotionally available to Ryan than his father had been to him. As Bill shared his struggles and aspirations with his father, he found opportunities to express some of these negative feelings with his family.

Of note, while I never saw Ryan in therapy with Bill and Lisa, this case nicely illustrates the connection between parts and wholes that began our chapter. When Bill and Lisa argued about parenting, each replayed individual themes that not only connected them to their families of origin but also were kept alive in their marriage. As Ryan witnessed the conflict, he became part of a triangle that would further influence his individual development. When Bill and Lisa began to work on their issues with their own families, they were also better able to remove Ryan from a triangulated position. We might argue that over time he had learned to play his mom against his dad to escape responsibility, as the family had numerous examples similar to the one in which he missed his SAT prep class. A traditional psychological view of the problems in the family would alternately focus on a manipulative, underachieving teenager; a depressed, critical, negative mother; and a passive-aggressive, emotionally unavailable father.

This case illustrates that putting this problem in a broader context helps us see both the truth and the limitations in these descriptions. By looking at the problem in context, the problems are more understandable and more difficult to simply pathologize. Further, using a Bowenian approach to the family of origin issues allowed each member of the couple to experience the validity of their own perspective, while also seeing the way that the perspective fit with the whole. Like the blind men with the elephant, Bill and Lisa were able to become even more expert at their part of the elephant, while also becoming more respectful of the expertise of the other.

To return to the general systems theory concept, the idea of context is ubiquitous and foundational. Understanding a problem in context means seeing all of the systems and subsystems in which a problem is embedded. Using the idea of multiple perspectives, we can see that our understanding of a problem will be limited by the systems in which we are embedded and can shift when the context shifts. This ability to use multiple perspectives provides numerous vantage points for addressing a problem. Further, the idea of nonsummativity turns our attention to parts and wholes, noting that the whole cannot be understood by simply summing the parts. Instead, using the idea of open systems, we can understand the creation of wholes and the relationship between parts and wholes by observing interactions. Perspectives such as Bowen's theory help us see that as individuals we are separate systems with unique identities who are also part of larger systems. This dynamic tension between parts and wholes means that systems are always moving targets, a phenomenon that we will revisit when we examine causality and change.

CHAPTER 3

Causality

WHEN MY DAUGHTER was only a month old, we took a trip from Chicago to Denver for my husband and I to interview for jobs. While we were in Denver, my grandmother died, and my daughter and I flew to New Mexico for the funeral. The day after we returned to Chicago, we spent the afternoon and evening at a good friend's wedding. Although my daughter was relatively easy to soothe and manage during all of this upheaval, for three days after we returned to our (relatively new) routine, my daughter cried for hours each day. I took her to the pediatrician after a couple of days, thinking that she had picked up some strange illness during our travels or that she was developing an atypical form of colic. The doctor was unable to find anything wrong and encouraged me to be patient. I'll never forget pondering all of this with my own therapist, expressing my frustration that I didn't know why my daughter was crying. His response was "You'll probably never know what was wrong." I was shocked by his reply! It was inconceivable that I could tolerate not knowing why my baby had been crying.

THE NEED TO KNOW WHY

Just as human beings seem programmed to try to organize our experiences into meaningful wholes, we are also hardwired to understand and explain why things happen. Our philosophical and scientific traditions are based on this ongoing quest to find the causes for events that we experience. When something happens, we want to know why. This process of learning about cause and effect starts early in our cognitive development and continues throughout the life span. Think of the baby in the high chair, repeatedly dropping her spoon from

33

the tray and watching it fall. Part of the scenario generally also includes watching the parent repeatedly return the spoon to the tray, so in this case, both brain development and positive reinforcement are encouraging the baby's physics experiment.

Our scientific method is designed to harness and organize our desire to understand causality. When we observe phenomena, we are asked to generate hypotheses that might explain what we have seen and then set up experiments to test the hypotheses we have generated. Based on the results of these experiments, we can revise our hypotheses and develop theories that further explain what we are observing. It is absolutely mind-boggling to consider all of the advances in technology, medicine, and a myriad of other areas that can ultimately be traced to this scientific method. Yet the method also has limitations, many of which come from some of the assumptions about its application.

In the last chapter, we looked at the ways that traditional laboratory science isolated and reduced phenomena when trying to address the problem of human obesity. As we saw, this practice can help us understand some aspects of systems functioning, yet it can also be misleading when it prevents us from looking at people and events in context. A similar problem exists when we look at causality. Traditional laboratory science looks for the best explanation for phenomena, which leads to an emphasis on singular causality. In addition, Western science views causality as a linear process. Like the baby in the high chair, we like to establish probability in a linear fashion, noting that if *a* happens, it will be followed by *b*. If I drop my spoon, it will fall to the floor.

While the predictability offered by this type of cause-and-effect thinking can be very reassuring, it has important drawbacks, as well. Another baby example comes to mind, this time with my son. When he was an infant, he was plagued with recurrent ear infections. He would be treated with one type of antibiotic and then recover, and then a few weeks later, he would be treated with a different antibiotic when the problem recurred. When he was 9 months old, we finally had tubes placed in his ears, yet he continued to get ear infections, and to be treated with antibiotics, for the next several months. I was complaining about the situation to a colleague whose partner was studying acupuncture, and he suggested that this treatment might help my son. Another colleague suggested that I needed to feed him yogurt and other foods that boost the immune system. We discontinued the antibiotics, started feeding him more yogurt (the only food on the list that he would eat), and took him to a pediatric acupuncture specialist.

Within a couple of weeks, his ears were clear, he did not get another ear infection for a full year, and the recurrent infections never returned.

I think that this story helps us understand the limits of our scientific method in different ways. If we start by looking at linear causality, then we have to ask what causes ear infections. Because we know that ear infections are caused by bacteria, then we know that the bacteria will be killed by an antibiotic. Our scientific method has yielded a simple and elegant solution to our problem on one level, but on another level, we see that the problem was not only not solved but instead became worse. The infection returned and needed another antibiotic. If we take a step back, we see a circular pattern: ear infection, antibiotic use, period of time without ear infection, ear infection, antibiotic use, and period of time without an ear infection.

As systems theory encourages us to look at the circular pattern, we inherently redefine the problem. Rather than stating that the problem is bacteria in the ear canal, which is the singular, linear explanation, we see that the problem is that the immune system cannot consistently manage the bacteria. If we look more at the relationship between my son's immune system and the bacteria, we will begin to look at the multiple causes for the immune system deficiency. In this instance, it now seems likely that the repeated antibiotic use actually inhibited his immune system, making it more likely that he would get sick in the future. Because of the limits of linear cause-and-effect thinking, it is not uncommon that some type of action will have unintended consequences. In this instance, the solution (antibiotic use) reinforced the problem (recurrent ear infections), an example of the type of well intentioned negative repercussion that we will explore more in later chapters, when we talk about change.

Once we start looking at multiple causality, we also have multiple avenues for intervention. In this case, we might say that I was a poor scientist because I started feeding my son yogurt and taking him to the acupuncturist at the same time. Do I know which of these interventions was actually effective? But because this experiment is taking place in an open system, it would be difficult to determine causality even if I had tried these interventions sequentially.

The systems pioneer Gregory Bateson used a much-cited example to look at the limitations of linear causality with living things (Bateson, 1972; Nichols & Schwartz, 2001). In the first instance, the group is instructed to set up an experiment to answer the following question: "What will happen when a woman kicks a rock?" We can predict that the force of the woman's kick will move the rock and that the precise distance will depend on the size of the rock and the strength of the kick. When the experiment is finished, the rock will stay where it was moved. Now the group is asked to stage another experiment to answer the question: "What will happen when a woman kicks a dog?" Prediction is much more difficult in this case and depends on a great deal more than the strength of the woman and the size of the dog. In addition, we would have a hard time identifying when the experiment is over. Imagine that the woman was nervous about kicking the dog and kicked him very lightly. The dog thought the woman wanted to play and began to nibble at her pant leg in return. The woman was fearful that the dog would bite her and tried to run away from the dog. As she ran, the dog chased her. The woman continued running and then started to scream. The woman turned, yelled at the dog, and gave the dog a harder kick. At that point, the dog bit her.

Bateson's example, which I have embellished, starts with showing the stark difference between the rock as subject and the dog as subject. The story highlights the fact that multiple variables contribute to our ability to predict outcomes, and it shows that a simple description of linear cause and effect is likely to leave out important information. Watzlawick discusses the fact that kicking the rock is an inherently linear process, as the energy from the kick is transferred to the rock. This type of linear energy transfer has long been studied in physics, but we see that kicking the dog represents an entirely different study. While some energy is transferred from the kick to the dog, numerous other processes are at work and influence the outcome (Watzlawick, Bavelas, & Jackson, 1967). In this example, we could summarize our experiment by saying that the woman kicked the dog, and the outcome was that the dog bit the woman. While these facts are true, this description leaves out the circular pattern that contributed to the behavior. Based on this example, we could certainly advise the woman not to kick dogs if she wanted to avoid being bitten, but if she wanted to learn more about how to get along with dogs, she could benefit from understanding the entire sequence.

WHO IS AT FAULT?

Although Bateson's example is a bit absurd, the predilection to lose valuable information through simple linear causality is rife in the mental health field. Consider Carol, a 44-year-old woman who was referred to me by her 13-year-old daughter's therapist, Samantha. Samantha said that the daughter, Emma, was struggling with issues of depression and self-esteem, but "given Carol's poor parenting skill, of course Emma struggles." Samantha experienced Carol as erratic and volatile, at times enthusiastic about Emma's growing competence and at other times hostile and undermining. She believed that Carol lacked the ability to empathize with Emma's experience, and therefore Emma was even more prone to hopelessness and depression than most 13-year-old girls. Samantha told me, "I can't get anywhere with this mom because she sees me as competition for Emma's affection. I haven't been able to get a good history from mom, but I'm sure that there is trauma or abuse there somewhere."

When Carol came to see me, she started by saying, "I'm sure you have heard all about what a bad mother I am from Samantha. I know she thinks I'm too hard on Emma, but I can tell that she has no clue about what it's like living with a moody 13-year-old." While her manner was somewhat brittle and negative, I was impressed by how accurately she summed up Samantha's perception, and I wondered if she knew that Samantha did not have children. When I went on to ask how Carol felt about coming to therapy, she said, "I don't really think this will help. I've tried therapy several times before, we always spend lots of time on my crappy childhood, and it never goes anywhere. But Emma really likes Samantha and knows that Samantha recommended that I come here. If I ask Emma to work on her issues, I guess I should, too."

We can easily see Samantha's assumptions in this case, and they are firmly grounded in psychological tradition. As Emma's therapist, there is a strong pull for her to become aligned with Emma's perspective. Samantha experiences Carol as interpersonally difficult and witnesses Emma's mood difficulties. Her implicit message is that Carol's difficult personality is the cause of Emma's struggles and, in turn, her difficult personality was caused by some kind of childhood trauma. Using this lens, the child's problem is always the fault of the parent; historically, usually the problem was blamed on the mother, but more recently, fathers have been included in this equation, even if only through their lack of involvement.

Given the prevalence of this lens, I often try to help my students understand how inevitable it is that parents will be anxious and defensive when they seek therapy with or for their children. Yet this case illustrates the dilemma faced by Samantha and by me as Carol's therapist. We are both hoping that Carol can use her therapy to become a better parent. Fortunately, the focus on multiple and circular causality helps us see that Carol can make constructive changes in her parenting without reinforcing the idea that Emma's problems are all her fault. And while this distinction between responsibility and blame may at first sound like semantics, in my experience this subtle but important distinction can be extremely therapeutic.

MANY PATHS TO THE SAME DESTINATION

Another systems concept that moves away from linear cause and effect is *equifinality*, which refers to the fact that the same outcome can be reached from different original conditions. As Bertalanffy points out, within a closed system the final result of an experiment can be predicted by the original condition, but in an open system, the result is the product of an interaction of variables. For example, when a child is having problems, it is easy to employ linear causality and say that a child's problems are the result of poor parenting. The principle of equifinality shows that a child's problem can result from a variety of starting points and that within an open system it is likely that several factors have contributed to the problem. This realization can both cut through defensiveness and help parents understand that improved parenting can be part of the solution to the child's problem.

To be more specific, Carol came to one session describing a difficult interaction she had with Emma. Emma came home from school complaining that two of her friends had decided to do a group project and did not include her. In trying to make Emma feel better, Carol told Emma that it would be easier to do the project by herself, rather than working with her friends. Emma was dejected, and when Carol tried to ask about her feelings, Emma simply said that her mother didn't understand her. Frustrated by Emma's increasing emotionality, Carol told her, "Well, maybe you should ask them why they didn't pick you. Last time you did a project with them, you didn't work very hard, so maybe they don't trust you anymore." While Carol's stated goal in giving Emma this feedback was to help her see that she could go back to her friends and promise them she would work harder, you can imagine that this wasn't the effect of her comments. Instead, Emma screamed at her, "You think I'm a terrible person! I knew it all along!" and ran to her room, crying.

In this instance, we see that Carol contributed to the problem by missing the chance to empathize with Emma's hurt feelings, and that if she had started there, she might have had the chance to help Emma solve her problem. Yet Emma gave Carol very little to work with, and certainly Emma's negativity and reactivity was part of the problem. Together they repeated the pattern of subtly invalidating each other.

Looking at the interaction in circular terms, each approached the other with the hope of making a connection, and when that hope was frustrated, they found indirect ways to attack the other. The more emotional and despondent Emma became the more incompetent and anxious Carol felt. She responded to this anxiety by trying to be businesslike, but not only did she miss Emma's feelings, she ultimately blamed Emma for the problem.

As we processed this example in session, Carol was able to see the challenges that Emma presented to her, as well as her own deficits in meeting the challenges. Rather than attributing the problem to her being a bad mother or Emma being a bad kid, she could see that in this inter-action they each triggered negative reactions in the other. As Carol examined her part of the pattern, she identified the ways that her own history made Emma's negative feelings especially difficult. Carol had experienced her own mother as frequently hostile and occasionally abusive. She had reacted to her mother's rejection and criticism by focusing on external achievements and keeping her distance emotionally.

Carol was determined to make Emma feel loved and accepted in a way that she did not experience with her mother, and it was very triggering for her to see Emma feel hurt or upset. As we worked together, she was able to understand that at times negative feelings were inevitable, but that these feelings could be accepted and worked with in a way that she had never experienced. Having this model allowed her to change her destructive behavior without blaming or punishing herself. At the same time, she could challenge Emma to behave differently without being so critical or negative. In this specific example, she went back and asked Emma to talk about her feelings more openly and directly. As Carol was able to focus on Emma's experience, she felt more confident as a parent and was therefore more accepting of herself and of Emma. Using this case, we can return to Bateson's example and understand that a focus on multiple causality was empowering to Carol. Instead of blaming the woman for being bitten by the dog (it is the parents' fault when children have problems) or assuming that dogs will be dogs (what do you expect from a teenager?), Carol looked at what she could influence in the situation and was ultimately less anxious and more effective.

BLAME AND RESPONSIBILITY

Issues of blame and responsibility have a long history in family systems work and deserve further discussion. Although family systems work developed in part in reaction to psychoanalytic models that were seen as overly mother-blaming, early family systems research on schizophrenia seemed to shift the cause from the mother to the family—while still maintaining a fairly linear, blaming stance. As we will see in the next chapter, when discussing communication, Bateson and the Palo Alto group noticed a particular type of problematic communication that existed in families with a schizophrenic member (Bateson, 1972, 1979; Nichols & Schwartz, 2001). As they observed and catalogued the now famous double-bind communications, they fell into the very nonsystemic trap of linear and singular causality. While the descriptions of double-bind communication highlight the statements of each member of the family, it is clear that the parent (usually the mother) creates the double bind that then causes the so-called crazy response of the schizophrenic.

Luckily, there are current conceptualizations of schizophrenic symptomatology that reflect both multiple and circular causality. Schizophrenia is thought to result from a combination of genetic predisposition and environmental stressors, which could include a variety of family or social problems. In addition, the level of functionality or adjustment can be increased by structured routines, medication, and social support. Current family treatments for schizophrenia highlight the importance of reducing negative expressed emotion, which highlights a circular causality model (C. M. Anderson, 1986). Within this model, families learn that as there is increased symptomatology in the system, family members may all experience greater anxiety and affect. If this affect is expressed directly, it is likely to exacerbate psychotic symptomatology, which in turn generates greater negative affect. By reducing these negative affective chains, families with schizophrenic members reduce distress as well as psychotic symptoms. Rather than blaming the family for the symptoms, this approach highlights the ways that family members can escape patterns of negatively triggering one another.

SHARED RESPONSIBILITY IS NOT EQUAL RESPONSIBILITY

Of course, multiple and circular causality does not imply equal responsibility for all problems, and family therapy has had to face numerous criticisms for the inappropriate application of ideas such as circular causality. Beginning in the late 1980s, Virginia Goldner and other feminist family therapists began writing about the ways that domestic violence had been ignored in the family therapy literature

(Goldner, 1985; Goldner, Penn, Sheinberg, & Walker, 1990). By focusing on the fact that both members of the couple contribute to the problem, the reality of unequal relational power was overlooked, at times leading to a blame-the-victim stance. While we will examine issues of power and privilege in more depth in later chapters, this distinction between contributing to a problem and being responsible for a problem can frequently be a useful clinical discussion. In the case of Carol and Emma, it was helpful to acknowledge Emma's contribution to their cycle, but as the parent in the system, Carol held more of the power and the responsibility for change.

There is a similar challenge in helping couples recover from affairs. To begin the healing process, it is frequently necessary for the person who had the affair to be fully accountable for betraying the relationship and causing the breach in trust (Pittman, 1989). By taking complete responsibility for having the affair, the partner who violated the relationship can begin to regain the trust of the wronged partner and in that process can often restore a sense of integrity in owning the wrongdoing. As the work continues, it may also involve looking at problems in the relationship for which both members were responsible. There is a delicate balance between allowing the affair partner to take responsibility for the affair and helping both partners own problems in the relationship.

One of the most interesting theoretical shifts in looking at causality can be seen in behavioral therapies. These theories were heavily grounded in the practice of basic science and many behavioral descriptions of events were extremely linear. Starting with classical conditioning, we see that Pavlov helped us understand how emotional reactions are conditioned through experience (Munger, 2003; Sheehy, 2004). Through the elegant simplicity of noticing that by pairing the sound of a bell with the pleasurable experience of being fed, the sound of the bell could then elicit the pleasurable sensation of anticipating food, leading to salivation. These scientific findings were quickly applied to humans, most famously in the 1920s by the psychologist John Watson (Sheehy, 2004). Watson was able to show that he could create a fear reaction in a small child where none had existed before.

Although current sensibilities question the famous experiment, Watson did contribute to our understanding of emotional learning in his work with Albert and the white rabbit. By pairing a frightening stimulus (loud noise) with an inherently pleasant object (a cuddly white rabbit), Watson conditioned the child to become afraid of the rabbit.

In contrast to the Freudian views of the day, which attributed emotions to internal, unconscious conflicts, the behavioral perspective looked at emotions as learned phenomena. According to this theory, we walk through the world accruing both pleasurable and aversive experiences, and this emotional learning helps us seek pleasure and avoid pain.

Skinner went further in looking at the ways that organisms operate on their environment to seek pleasure and avoid pain (Sheehy, 2004). Working first with pigeons, he noted that any behavior that was followed by a reward was likely to be repeated, behaviors that were followed by something painful were less likely to be repeated, and behaviors that received no reinforcement whatsoever were eventually dropped. Again, applying these ideas of operant conditioning to humans, Skinner saw human behavior as the product of contingencies in the environment (Skinner, 1974). Like classical conditioning, the mechanism for behavior change is direct and linear. To develop a desired behavior, first find a way to elicit the desired behavior, reinforce the behavior intermittently when it occurs, and expect that the behavior will be repeated. To eliminate an undesirable behavior, remove all reinforcement for the behavior, if possible, and wait for it to be extinguished. If the reinforcement cannot be removed, the behavior should be punished so that it will be discontinued temporarily, allowing a more desirable behavior to be reinforced in its place.

While operant and classical conditioning have had utility as foundational principles, other theorists have expanded these theories to make them more applicable to human behavior. Although he isn't generally considered a systems theorist, Albert Bandura elaborated on Skinner's operant conditioning by examining reinforcement schedules in a relational context (Bandura, 1977; Sheehy, 2004). Calling his approach *social learning theory*, Bandura was able to highlight the ways that the type of pleasure and pain that is meaningful to human beings generally occurs in the context of relationships. While traditional stimulus/response behavioral approaches often focused on tangible reinforcement, Bandura saw that humans learned by watching each other and that approval and rejection could be powerful sources of pleasure and pain.

EXPLAINING VICIOUS CYCLES

In the 1970s, couples and family therapists began to combine systemic and behavioral principles, an effort that has continued to the present. One of the best known of this group, Gerald Patterson (1971), started with applying operant conditioning and social learning theory principles to problem behavior in children. Patterson and his group methodically analyzed the reinforcement schedules of children in their practice and began to elaborate the circular patterns that kept problem behaviors in place. A traditional behavioral approach focused on the ways that parents reinforce their children for undesired behavior, generally by ignoring positive behavior and giving intense attention to negative behavior. But Patterson and his group took these ideas forward in a couple of ways. First, in social contexts, behaviors simultaneously serve as stimuli and reinforcement, so that a behavior will elicit a response from another family member, and this response will elicit a subsequent behavior. Rather than a linear stimulus-response pattern, we see an ongoing and mutual cycle of people shaping each other's behavior.

Second, Patterson recognized that operant and classical conditioning go hand in hand in these situations. He pointed out that when negative behavioral cycles persist, family members become aversive stimuli for one another (Patterson, 1970). The classical conditioning that occurs further solidifies the operant conditioning; for example, as parents feel upset by their child's behavior, they feel anger and anxiety, and the mere presence of the child elicits a painful negative emotion. Trying to avoid that feeling, parents keep an emotional distance from the child that is also experienced negatively by the child. When given requests or directives, the child is not motivated by a positive relationship to comply. Instead, the request is perceived negatively and ignored until the parent becomes frustrated enough to pay a great deal of attention to the child. When the parent is acting in some extreme manner, the child finally complies. This prototypical example shows that the parent has trained the child to ignore requests initially (reinforcing the behavior after many requests), while the child has trained the parent to go to extremes to get his attention. In addition, the outcome of this cycle is that each party feels anxious and upset in the presence of the other. Patterson points out that the key behavioral efficacy that each party has in this cycle is aversive control (Patterson, 1993). Parents and children are joined in their ability to make each other miserable!

As I mentioned in the first chapter, because I started my career as an elementary school teacher, I felt well-versed in behavioral principles, which I applied in a linear manner (star charts on the desks of my students) to very good effect. When I returned to graduate school to study clinical psychology, I was drawn to psychodynamic theories, and I was somewhat dismayed to learn that in the integrative model I was taught through my systems training, I would have to implement behavioral theories, which in my mind did not address the deeper truth of human suffering.

From this perspective, I had the good fortune of being supervised on a family case that helped me appreciate the depth of the systemic behaviorism developed by Patterson and his colleagues. Pia was a 10-year-old girl who was brought to therapy by her parents, Roberta and Gillian, for a recent increase in noncompliant behavior. Roberta had recently been laid off from her job in marketing and had been working from home for the past six months. Both parents felt that an increase in Roberta's availability in the home would be positive for Pia, who had always struggled in minor ways with small acts of compliance, such as keeping her room clean and keeping up with homework. But instead of improving, Pia's behavior had steadily worsened since Roberta had been working from home. Although she was extremely bright, her grades were only mediocre and had dropped in the past few months. She seemed to enjoy upsetting Gillian with minor behavioral violations, such as belching at the table and wearing dirty clothes. Even more distressing to Gillian, Pia was resisting activities that they used to enjoy together, such as craft projects and board games, and instead repeatedly requested that she be allowed to do these things with only Roberta.

Gillian and Roberta were in general agreement about their standards for Pia's behavior, but Gillian tended to be the enforcer of these standards, while Roberta was more easygoing and thought that Pia would gradually come around. When I explored the strategies they used to address Pia's behavior, Gillian employed frequent reminders and complained when Pia did not comply, while Roberta was inclined to leave the task of disciplining Pia to Gillian. Not surprisingly, Roberta felt that Gillian was overly harsh and critical of Pia, and Gillian felt that Roberta was weak and indulgent. It was a relief to both to see that their standards were similar and to hear that together they could teach Pia to maintain these behaviors, although this teaching would involve changes for both of them.

CREATING POSITIVE CYCLES

We started with a behavioral plan to encourage Pia to do her homework, clean her room, and clear the table after dinner. Knowing that positive reinforcement provides the best way to establish good habits, we set up a plan by which Pia would earn points each day for doing 30 minutes of homework, making her bed, getting her clothes in the hamper, and taking the dinner dishes to the sink. Pia was neutral about these tasks initially, saying that they weren't hard but weren't really important, but she became more invested when we looked at positive reinforcement for completing them. Pia had been asking to be allowed to watch *The Simpsons* on television and to sleep on the pull-out couch in the living room. Gillian worried that Bart Simpson would be a negative influence on Pia's behavior, but Roberta felt that they could watch the show together and change the reward if indeed Pia started to copy Bart's negative behaviors. Both parents wanted to stay away from material rewards, and I agreed with them completely. We also determined that Pia would earn 10 minutes of additional computer time for meeting the target behavior each day, so that she had both immediate and cumulative rewards. As is typical in this type of work, developing the behavioral plan also required the family to improve their communication skills, as they were more accustomed to arguing and avoiding difficult topics than to listening to one another and solving problems together.

Although it isn't always the case, in this instance the behavioral plan worked like a charm. All the family members were skeptical about the other's ability to change: Pia thought Gillian would be unwilling to follow through with rewards; Gillian thought Roberta would reward Pia whether or not she did the work, and Roberta thought that both Gillian and Pia would be unable to change. When we look at circular causality, however, we see that as each member made small changes, the entire pattern could change in a larger way. Roberta bought into the behavioral plan and began attending to Pia's compliance. She also appreciated Gillian's willingness to employ positive reinforcement. Gillian felt Roberta's investment and was relieved to have her help. Pia experienced less tension between her parents, as well as more power and competence through earning rewards than through upsetting Gillian.

As we continued monitoring the family progress in therapy, we moved on to address the subtler problem of the increased distance between Pia and Gillian. While Pia's behavior was significantly better and all family members were happy with their progress, Pia continued to refuse to do activities with Gillian, which was very disappointing to Gillian. Because they had always enjoyed doing craft projects together, we decided to spend a session making individual and group collages in order to understand how their positive time together could work better. As we were all thumbing through magazines and making small talk, Pia went right to work. She found a picture of an attractive brunette in profile, attached it to a poster board, and then cut out the letters "n-o-n-o-n-o-n-o" to come out of the woman's mouth. Gillian watched intently and asked the obvious question, "Is that me?" Pia coyly said, "Yes!" I was worried that Gillian would become defensive, and Roberta looked tense and unhappy. To our surprise, Gillian was able to ask Pia about her perception of all the restrictions that were placed on her, and she reassured Pia that she also didn't want to be the "all no" mother. As Roberta saw that there wasn't going to be a conflict between Pia and Gillian, she relaxed and noted that if she said no more frequently, Gillian could be more flexible. Pia explained that she never wanted to hear no from either parent, and although this comment rubbed Gillian the wrong way, with a little help from me, both parents were able to respect Pia's comment without feeling that it undermined their authority.

Behavioral theory can help us understand what happened between Pia and her parents, and a systemic application of behavioral theory gives an even more complete picture. When both parents reinforced the target behavior and ignored her negative attitude (operant conditioning), Pia's nondesired behavior was fairly quickly extinguished and replaced. This happened in a circular fashion: Pia's compliance reinforced her parents for being warmly structuring, rather than her resistance reinforcing Roberta's avoidance and Gillian's nagging. In addition, a change in classical conditioning occurred. The positive behaviors created a calmer, more relaxed atmosphere that replaced the anxious, resentful tone in the house. Again in a circular fashion, as Gillian was less critical and vigilant, Roberta was more engaged and involved. As this shift occurred in the parents, Pia was less pulled to Roberta and less avoidant of Gillian. All family members began to look forward to their time together, rather than avoiding and dreading their time at home.

Similar to the way that an understanding of circular causality helped each family member change the cycle, the systemic emphasis on multiple causality was very helpful in this case. As is typical in most family cases, each family member initially saw the others as the problem. Gillian actively blamed Roberta's easygoing attitude, Pia blamed Gillian's negativity, and Roberta wanted to deny that there was a problem. Starting with multiple definitions of the problem allowed the family to move away from the kind of finger-pointing that was so painful for all of them.

While I've chosen to focus on Patterson's behavioral family therapy (Patterson, 1993) as a good example of the systemic view of circular causality, numerous other examples exist. John Gottman's foundational research on couple interactions, based on a behavioral perspective, highlights the way that behavioral sequences can become ingrained (Gottman & Gottman, 2008). In several well-replicated studies, Gottman documents the importance of the balance between positive and negative interactional cycles. Again highlighting the complementary nature of operant and classical conditioning, Gottman notes that positive and negative affective cycles tend to be self-reinforcing. In addition, Gottman stresses the power of negative interactional cycles. Overall, it takes five positive interactions to counteract the effect of one negative interaction. Gottman's more recent work helps us understand why couples can become so stuck in either positive or negative cycles. He notes that in happy couples, a negative interaction frequently does not start a negative cycle. He calls this phenomenon the ability to up-regulate positive affect during conflict. We could easily apply this concept to our family case: When the ratio of positive interactions has significantly increased, we will assume that each family member will be conditioned to appreciate and enjoy the presence of the other. In the context of these positive feelings, Gillian may still experience an initial feeling of annoyance when Pia misbehaves, but the positive feelings will override her initial negative reaction. This override stops the negative cycle that would have occurred a few weeks before.

According to the core concept, early applications of systems theory to psychology emphasized the prevalence of both multiple and circular causality. This model counteracts the very human tendency to look for single, linear explanations for behavior. The movement beyond linear causality can correct mistakes that occur from a narrow focus on single causes and offer a greater breadth of intervention strategies.

Further, in my experience, the emphasis on multiple and circular causality is a huge component of successful therapy because it replaces blame with responsibility. This shift from shame and defensiveness to genuine regret and accountability is equally helpful in working with individuals, couples, or families. Most of us harbor primitive and profound wishes to be completely blameless in our life's problems and simultaneously fear that we are totally at fault for our own misery. To be able to step back and acknowledge that there are numerous contributors to our problems takes the idea of context a step further. As my husband has pointed out to me in the midst of an argument, "You teach systems theory, so you know that it is unlikely that the problem is *all* my fault." By recognizing multiple contributions to a problem, we can move away from a posture of blame to create an atmosphere of understanding and problem solving. In addition, by adding the concept of circular causality, we see that frequently the pattern created in a negative cycle keeps a problem locked in place. To be able to say, "You have developed a pattern in which you bring out the worst in each other" is not only less blaming; it also offers a focus on problem behavior rather than problem people. As we will see in the next chapter, many of those problem behaviors revolve around communication.

CHAPTER 4

Communication

I TEACH A seminar to doctoral students in which we work with couples and families, and a few years ago we decided, as a joke, that we would never accept a couple's case that didn't list communication difficulties as one of their presenting problems. The joke got old very quickly, because every single couple that came through our clinic described communication issues as one of their major difficulties. As therapists, we know that communication problems are rampant when there is distress in a relationship, but when we say that a couple or family has communication problems, do we know what that means?

We may have a general sense that when someone has communication problems, the individual is having a hard time feeling heard or understood. She may yell and fight rather than resolving problems, or he may avoid discussing difficult or emotional issues. Yet stating that there is a communication problem doesn't give us specific information about the difficulty and it certainly doesn't tell us how to intervene. From my experience, communication theory is one of the areas in which systems theory is so incredibly helpful. The ability to analyze communication problems on multiple levels and then to replace destructive communication with more constructive communication is one of the hallmarks of systems theory. In spite of what you may hear in the popular media, the task of reworking communication is often more difficult and more complex than it initially appears.

OBSERVING COMMUNICATION

One of the major contributors to a systemic view of communication is Paul Watzlawick (Watzlawick, Weakland, & Fisch, 1974). As mentioned earlier, his *Pragmatics of Human Communication*, published in 1967, summarized some of the work that Watzlawick did with Gregory Bateson and the Palo Alto group in the early 1960s (Watzlawick, Bavelas, & Jackson, 1967). Watzlawick, who died in 2007, was a psychologist who studied families with psychotic members and was especially interested in the analysis of human relationships. In looking at human communication, Watzlawick noted "the impossibility of not communicating" (Watzlawick, Bavelas, & Jackson, 1967, p. 48). Watzlawick notes the omnipresent and ubiquitous nature of human communication in this statement, in that all of our actions or inactions convey some type of meaning, which will be interpreted by those around us. Systems theory takes a step back to observe the cycles of communication that constitute the message sent and the message received, and this type of observation is known as metacommunication. Metacommunication examines the actual act of communication, and is a common thread in the practice of psychotherapy. As the therapist examines the metacommunication, or communicates about the communication, it is also helpful to distinguish between process and content. Process and content are different, and a metacommunication perspective helps to elucidate the ways that process and content can work together to create constructive communication.

Watzlawick illustrates the fact that human communication involves a message being sent and a message being received. Numerous factors influence both the sent and received messages. One way of examining these messages is to look at the difference between the *report function* of a communication and the *command function* of a communication. As Watzlawick used these terms, he noted how our decoding of messages is always influenced by context. The report function is the literal, face-value meaning of a communication. It is the surface level of meaning, and in verbal communication, it involves semantics. In contrast, the command function involves the latent content of communication. The command function is based on the relationship between the parties involved in the communication, and it includes the nonverbal cues that help the receiver encode the full meaning of the sender's message. The report function is generally thought of as the explicit message being expressed, and the command function describes the implicit message, especially the implicit message about the relationship between the sender and receiver.

Looking at both functions of communication shows us that we constantly, and usually unconsciously, weave together the report and the command to translate messages around us. If my 15-year-old son says to me, "Mom, you are a great driver," I could take this message literally and accept the words on their face value. Knowing more about the context of the relationship, however, I would tune in to the fact that my son has his driver's permit, he likes to show off, and he loves sarcasm. In this case, the report function of the communication indicated that he is giving me a compliment, but the command function of the communication suggests that he is either teasing or insulting me (which may be the same thing with 15-year-old sons).

When I think of the difference between the report and command functions of communication, I can never forget a personal example that provided a vivid illustration of the difference between the two levels. I was standing outside a Paris nightclub with a (former) partner. It was a beautiful evening, and we were waiting to go inside and listen to some jazz. The dialogue went something like this:

MY PARTNER: "You should buy that Miles Davis album I told you about."

MY RESPONSE: (incredulous) "I can't believe you would say that to me!" (I turn away, angry tears in my eyes.)

HIS RESPONSE: (rolling his eyes) "You're going to get mad at me for this? That's ridiculous!"

You can see that so far the conversation doesn't really make sense. Without more contextual information, we can only guess at my negative reaction. Did he forget that I don't like Miles Davis? Do I believe that he is insensitive to my financial issues? Did I tell him that I wanted him to buy me this album as a gift?

With more background, you would know that we had just finished a conversation processing the way that I felt invisible and inferior in our relationship because my partner was always being the expert and telling me what to do. I thought that I had sincerely and convincingly shown him examples of how I experienced him as controlling and condescending. The fact that my partner repeated the dynamic that we had just discussed illustrated an unchanging dynamic to me and suggested that the command function of his communication was to continually put me in my place. At the same time, he experienced my communication as irrational, unfair, and overly sensitive. The command function of my communication was that he needed to walk on eggshells and didn't have room to make mistakes. Returning to the issue of circular causality, you can see that with this type of communication, we were likely to reinforce both negative views and negative experiences of each other. The report function ensured that I experienced his comments as dominating and judgmental and that he experienced my reaction as irrational and petty.

MESSAGE SENT AND MESSAGE RECEIVED

This example also illustrates another set of communication constructs, the difference between intent and impact. In my experience, because we often confuse the two ideas, we often end up arguing about whether someone has a right to an emotional reaction. Even if my partner did not intend to insult me, the impact that I felt at his reaction was real, and there was no benefit in trying to deny the way that his comment hurt me. Understanding communication more fully allows us to separate intent and impact, which can clarify misunderstandings.

You can see that if we had not been so rigidly mired in the command function of the communication, we might have been able to repair our misunderstanding, and part of that reparation might have involved separating intent from impact. If I could have used better communication, I could have let him know that the way he phrased the statement felt condescending and that I wished he would have actively shown me that he perceived me as an equal. He could have responded with curiosity or empathy. The dialogue could have been repaired:

MY REACTION: "Yeah, I know that I'm overreacting, but when you make that kind of statement I feel like you are acting like my boss again. It feels awful, especially after the talk we just had."

HIS RESPONSE: "Wow, that's not what I meant, but I can see how you would feel that way. I was thinking of how much you would like some of the songs, but I can see how you felt that once again I was telling you what to do."

MY RESPONSE: "Sometimes it would be nice if you asked me about the music I have been listening to, instead of just telling me what I should listen to."

HIS REACTION: "Yeah, I'll try to do that more. It helps when you tell me this instead of just getting mad."

Of course, this dialogue happened only in my fantasy. Our actual dynamic felt so stuck to me that I ended the relationship a couple of days after this dialogue. I'm still not convinced that he didn't intend to take the upper hand with this type of exchange, but regardless of his contribution to the problem, I know that at the time I didn't have the ability to change my piece of the cycle. Ironically, I went home and purchased the Miles Davis album, which went on to become one of my all-time favorites.

FUNCTIONS OF COMMUNICATION

Yet another way of looking at communication difficulties is to examine the goals of communication. Within human relationships, communication can be used to solve problems or to create emotional connections. While both purposes of communication are legitimate, problems can occur when partners differ in how they value each function. I often find some of the descriptions of gender-based communication overly simplistic, but like most stereotypes, there is some truth to the idea that in our culture, males and females communicate differently. According to gender stereotypes, men typically use verbal communication to establish status or to solve problems, and women use verbal communication to create social bonds (Tannen, 2001). Regardless of whether the gender explanation makes sense to you, I imagine that you can find numerous examples of the difference between problem-solving communication and connecting communication. Of course, these types of communication are not mutually exclusive, as often good problem solving creates bonds, and emotional connections promote better problem solving. Yet in my clinical work, this distinction helps me understand the way that couples and families are often completely out of sync with one another, talking with two different agendas without even realizing that they are unwittingly working at cross purposes.

CORRECTING MISUNDERSTANDINGS

There is a substantial body of literature on the benefits of teaching communication skills to couples to prevent the kinds of misunderstandings I described (Markman, Stanley, & Blumberg, 1994). The cornerstone of this approach involves teaching the speaker–listener technique, which aims to maximize the chance that the message sent by the speaker will be the same as the message received by the partner. Skills training for the speaker focus on helping each member of the couple take responsibility for what is said to the partner, so that messages are clear, short, and understandable. Similarly, the listener is taught to put aside his own agenda temporarily in order to understand, and then paraphrase, the speaker's message. The speaker and listener make the commitment to adhere to their respective roles until the speaker feels that the message was understood, and then the roles are reversed. One goal of developing these communication skills and strategies is to limit destructive conflict and replace conflict with problem resolution.

Studies generally show that this type of skills training is most effective at preventing problems (Markman, 1993), and couples often complain that it feels artificial or contrived to use these techniques. Yet I often find it interesting to witness just how difficult it is for individuals to accurately state their positions and then correctly comprehend a partner's message. Thinking about communication from a systems perspective, it makes sense that there are a number of ways that communication can go awry, and it seems inevitable that a therapist will need a variety of tools to help couples communicate effectively. It is incredibly useful to know how to slow down the communication sufficiently to clarify each person's basic intent. When the goal of communication is to resolve conflict, it is essential that each side of a conflict is correctly identified and understood. When the goal of communication is emotional connection as well as problem solving, the opportunities for miscommunication increase even further.

Consider an unresolved argument that my clients Jim and Amy brought to their therapy session. Jim called Amy at work one afternoon and said, "Hey, what are you thinking for dinner tonight? I was thinking that bruschetta sounded good." Amy answered, "I haven't thought that far ahead; now that you ask, steak sounds good." He answered, "Well, you know that tomatoes are in season, and I can't stop thinking about bruschetta." Without much enthusiasm, she said, "Oh that sounds okay." He replied, "I may get off a little early, so I will see you at home." Jim and Amy have a nice garden and he's a great cook, so he decided to make the world's best bruschetta. He stopped by their favorite bakery for special bread to grill, and he used their best olive oil. The tomatoes were perfectly ripe, and Jim believed that he was making the dinner of Amy's dreams. When Amy arrived home from work, Jim said, "I have a surprise for you. How about some bruschetta?" Amy answered dejectedly, "I thought I told you I wanted steak!" Then the fight began in earnest, because they were both hurt and upset. He said to her, "I came home early just to make you bruschetta! I put all this work into making a nice meal for you. I wanted to make you happy. You don't have the capacity to appreciate me." To which she replied, "I didn't ask you to do this for me! I didn't ask for any of this. You asked me what I wanted, and I said steak. You don't care what I want. This is another example of your selfishness!"

MISSING THE BOAT

This clinical example illustrates the potential for miscommunication on a number of different levels. When Jim called Amy and asked what she wanted for dinner, the report function of the communication was literally to learn what she was in the mood to eat. But we know from the suggestion about the bruschetta, and from Jim's later comment about leaving work early, that the command function of the communication was to say, "I have something planned for dinner, and I hope that you enjoy it." Further, he seems to be saying, "I want you to feel loved when you eat my food, and I want you to love me for being such a good cook." In response, the command function of her communication seems to say, "I won't give you a lot of information, and I want you to care enough about me to listen very carefully and take me seriously." Already we see that the conflict between these levels of communication is sending a mixed message to Amy. In turn, Amy doesn't address the mixed message directly, but instead first responds only to the report function ("I want steak"). When Jim goes further in mentioning the bruschetta, Amy provides her own mixed message by agreeing to his request, without enthusiasm. The report function, "Bruschetta is fine," contrasts with the command function, "If you love me you will respect my desire for steak." In this case, Jim accepts the report function and misses the context of the command function.

At this point, Jim and Amy each blame the other for the miscommunication (You asked me what I wanted! You said bruschetta was okay!), and yet the underlying message has yet to be explored. If we look at Jim's intent, he was hoping to treat his wife to something that sounded wonderful to him. He intended to make her feel special, and he was hoping to receive admiration and appreciation in return. In turn, Amy responded to Jim's question by saying what she wanted. She intended to have her wishes heard and validated. In both cases, the intent did not match the impact. Jim's efforts in making the bruschetta didn't make Amy feel special but instead made her feel disregarded and ignored. Amy's insistence on her desire for steak didn't help Jim understand or respect her but instead made him feel unappreciated. Finally, in contrast to our predictions of gender-based communication, Jim called Amy (and made the bruschetta) out of a desire for connection. He didn't call to solve the problem of what to make for dinner; he called because he wanted to share his plan for creating a nice evening. Amy didn't feel the connection and instead saw the problem solving gone awry. If he called to ask what she wanted for dinner, then why didn't he show her the courtesy of sticking with the conversation and coming up with a mutually satisfying entrée?

DESTRUCTIVE COMMUNICATION

When we look back at early applications of communication principles, we see that Watzlawick and Bateson worked from the hypothesis that problematic communication causes both symptomatology and distress (Watzlawick, Bavelas, & Jackson, 1967). They studied interactions of families with a member suffering from schizophrenia in depth, examining both verbal and nonverbal exchanges. They identified a type of communication that was seen to be common in these families and thought to be so distressing that it caused psychotic symptoms. They called this communication a double bind. While double binds have since been described in slightly different ways by other systems theorists, Bateson described a double bind as having three key components: First, the communication must occur in an emotionally important, connected relationship. Second, there must be a conflict between the meaning of the report function of the communication and the meaning of the command function of the communication. Third, the rules of the system must be specific that the mixed message can't be addressed directly. This type of communication sets up the proverbial "stuck between a rock and a hard place" kind of feeling, since the discrepancy between the levels of communication is felt but must be denied, as the relationship is too important to just leave. It is worth noting that the act of therapy is designed to surface and address mixed messages. The act of exposing the conflict doesn't resolve the conflict, but an open acknowledgment of the conflict in itself defuses the double bind.

Bateson and Watzlawick noted that double-bind communication often preceded an increase in psychotic behavior, and they speculated that this type of communication caused schizophrenia (Bateson, 1972; Nichols & Schwartz, 2001; Watzlawick, Bavelas, & Jackson, 1967; Watzlawick, Weakland, & Fisch, 1974). Their logic seems strangely nonsystemic in some ways, as it implies a single cause for the problem (communication causes psychosis). Further, some of their examples of double-bind communication seem almost as linear and mother-blaming as the Freudian theories that they purported to replace (Nichols, 2010). For example, they describe a mother and father visiting their son in a mental hospital on Mother's Day. The son had been less symptomatic and had been able to get a pass to the infirmary to buy his mother a card. She opened the card, and the message inside said, "You have been like a mother to me." The mother was visibly upset by this message because, of course, she was his mother and was not "like a mother" to him. She began to cry, but when the son asked what was wrong, she said, "Nothing, I'm glad you think I am like a mother to you." The son knew that his mother was upset but didn't understand why. When he pressed further, she became angry and stated, "I am here to visit you, not to talk about myself," effectively ending the opportunity to process the communication further. At this point, the son became quite agitated and described his fear that poisonous gas was being piped in through the vents. The visit ended with the son appearing actively psychotic. The implication was that after the mother's rejection of the son's card and the family's inability to process this rejection, the son's psychotic symptoms actually made sense.

In this age of biologically based psychiatry, it seems almost quaint to think that communication could actually cause schizophrenia, but the example does highlight the way that communication can cause distress and the way that constructive communication could have potentially relieved distress. The act of attending therapy is inherently geared to addressing double binds by directly challenging the prohibition against confronting the mixed message. If the case would have been a family therapy case rather than a research case, we can guess that the therapist would have helped the mother express her disappointment in the son's card in a way that was less hostile and reactive. Of course, we might also examine the intent of the communication of the son in choosing the card—was he trying to express his ambivalence toward his mother with the message in the card? A key theme in the importance of good communication is that expressing ambivalence directly, rather than acting it out, has more positive, manageable results.

Current research on family therapy for schizophrenic symptoms suggests that Watlawick and Bateson were on to something important, although slightly different from what they described. The work of Carol Anderson (1986) and that of Ian Faloon (Faloon, Leff, Lopez-Ibor, May, & Okaska, 2005) have examined the interactions of families with members who have been diagnosed with schizophrenia. As mentioned earlier, their research validates the hypothesis that high levels of expressed emotion are likely to increase psychotic symptomatology. Their research programs have demonstrated the efficacy of teaching family members to reduce escalating emotional communication when psychotic members are agitated or distressed. If we go back to the issue of double-bind communication, we see that mixed messages create agitation, and the inability to address the mixed message directly escalates the negative emotion. The painful, stuck, mutually under-mining cycle established through the double bind is not unlike the aversive behavioral sequence described by Patterson (1971) and other behavioral systems theorists, as discussed in the last chapter. However, by looking at levels of communication that occur within the interaction, we have another way of understanding how these cycles are created and maintained.

ENHANCING AUTHENTICITY

There is a long tradition within the practice of family therapy of trying to restore family relationships by changing communication patterns. Although their styles of practicing therapy appear very different, both Carl Whitaker (1977) and Virginia Satir (1972) were influential family therapy pioneers who emphasized the healing power of emotional expression. As we are all influenced by our historical context, both Whitaker and Satir were heavily influenced by the humanistic-existential zeitgeist of the 1960s. When I show videos of Whitaker and Satir to my students now, they are outraged by the lack of boundaries, and they raise issues about the ethics of saying blatantly outrageous things to clients, or of hugging clients. These concerns are clearly valid, and there is no question that an unexamined and impul-sive use of emotion simply for the sake of catharsis can have negative consequences. When we look at the principles behind the experiential work of Satir and Whitaker, however, we see they were able to identify and rework inconsistent and conflictual communication in a way that was authentic and compelling. Further, the foundations of this expe-riential approach have been expanded in Greenberg and Johnson's emotionally focused therapy, a well-researched approach that we'll discuss later in the chapter (Greenberg, 2002; Johnson, 2002).

Like Murray Bowen and Salvador Minuchin, Carl Whitaker was trained as a psychiatrist during the late 1940s and worked with patients with chronic mental illness (Nichols & Schwartz, 2001). All of these family therapy pioneers expressed dissatisfaction with the psycho-dynamic orthodoxy of that time, and Whitaker was especially con-temptuous of the traditional application of Freudian theory. In fact, Whitaker rejected the idea that theory was useful in the practice of therapy (1976), instead seeing the use of theory as a way to become distant from experience. In an almost pure expression of communica-tion theory, Whitaker believed that being genuine and honest in the moment was the ultimate healing force, and he strove to jolt his clients out of their complacency and emotional dishonesty. Although he would reject a Freudian explanation of these forces, he did believe that human beings are socialized to deny their authentic feelings and that this socialization results in people being at war with themselves. This unexpressed internal conflict could cause a whole variety of individual symptoms and interpersonal problems. Whitaker felt that family beliefs and expectations constrained individuals from being true to themselves and that problems were compounded when families didn't know how to express or resolve conflict (Whitaker, 1981). For Whitaker, human relationships were inherently passionate and therefore naturally full of conflict, competition, and hatred, as well as joy and excitement. It is in denying and turning away from these intense feelings that we create problems for ourselves and for our families, according to Whitaker.

As a therapist, Whitaker was described as brash, blunt, and outrageous. He ran the psychotherapy clinic at the University of Wisconsin for 30 years. Not coincidentally, he typically worked with a cotherapist, most notably the talented clinician Gus Napier. Napier and Whitaker (1978) had a kind of good cop–bad cop approach, where Napier could be the more conventional therapist and help clients process and work through some of Whitaker's unconventional and often upsetting remarks. Whitaker professed an affinity for the absurd and was able to use his offbeat style to highlight the irony of the alienation that results from family disharmony. For example, Whitaker might say to an adolescent early in an interview, "How does it feel to know that your dad is a cripple?" when he explored the father's fight with polio and the son's difficulty with his father. Then Whitaker would stand back and, with the help of the cotherapist, watch where the pieces landed. The hope with this type of intervention was that the family could have a more honest conversation about the unexpressed anger, rejection, and resentment that were being surfaced through the adolescent's symptoms.

Virginia Satir's (1972) style was very different, yet she also worked from the premise that unexpressed feelings and issues were the root of human suffering. Satir was trained as a social worker and worked in Palo Alto with Bateson, Haley, and Watzlawick. Satir was also heavily influenced by the human potential movement of the 1960s, and she embraced humanistic theories that focused on actualization and other progressive ideas. In many ways, it is possible to see Satir and Whitaker as two sides of the same coin, with Whitaker highlighting the problems with repressed negative affect and Satir celebrating the healing power of warm, loving communication (Satir, 1983). As a therapist, Satir practically oozed empathy, and some of her techniques seemed to almost parody our notions of using affect in therapy. In one family therapy video, she holds the hand of a mute, disengaged adolescent and intones, "Your hand is soft and warm. I like holding it. Your hand feels very nice to me." While this focus on human affection might seem contrived, for Satir the emphasis on the unexpressed need for compassion, validation, and appreciation is almost always beneficial. In the case of the adolescent girl, the direct physical affection first caused the daughter to become more symptomatic in the session, which then allowed Satir to invite the parents to become more involved in their daughter's care.

COMMUNICATION BUILDS ATTACHMENT

While Whitaker and Satir both focused on direct, affect-rich communication, more recent applications of experiential approaches emphasize a stronger theoretical underpinning. In different ways, Whitaker and Satir focused on feeling more than on ideas, to the point of seeing theories as tools for creating distance and empty intellectualization. Again, these criticisms may apply to certain applications of psychological theory, but there is nothing in systems theory that says that good communication is affective rather than logical in nature. Instead, a current application of systems theory is seen in the work of Sue Johnson (2004, 2002), who uses attachment theory as the basis for her experiential approach. Rather than rejecting theory as limiting, Johnson draws on both theory and research to help us understand the richness of human communication and to correct the potential pitfalls involved in pursuing affect in naive, exaggerated ways.

According to Johnson, attachment is a primary human need, as basic as the need for food and water. Human beings are hardwired for attachment, as being in caring and involved attachment relationships is necessary for our survival. The primary means of developing, maintaining, and repairing our attachment relationships comes through our experience of affect and can be seen in the way that affect is communicated. An enormous body of research elucidates the development of attachment relationships between infants and their caretakers. It is now well documented that the bond between an infant and her caretaker develops through interactions that take place between them. As the caregiver feeds, changes, holds, and gazes at the infant, the infant experiences a sense of well-being, feeling both calmed and soothed by this positive attention. In turn, the infant's response to the caregiver can create a reciprocal positive experience. As the baby is calmed and soothed, the caregiver experiences a sense of efficacy and competence in providing love and care to the infant. When this circular interaction goes well, both parties create a positive, safe, and responsive environment for the other.

Of course, any interaction is going to include problems, and part of what attachment theory helps us understand is the mechanism for reconnecting when there has been a rupture in the attachment. Even when the infant is very young, there will be times when the connection feels too close or too intense, and the baby will need to turn away from the comfort of the caregiver. Similarly, the caregiver sometimes disappoints the baby by being less responsive or available than the baby needs. The ability to tolerate the frustration inherent in these moments of broken connection is at the root of developing a truly secure attachment. However, it is just these small breaks in connection that can sometimes cause more extreme reactions and lead to insecure attachments. For example, when a parent overreacts to a baby's need for a break or for space, the parent may actually feel a sense of rejection from the baby. In this case, the parent's hurt or anger is experienced by the baby as disapproval, which then causes internal discomfort for the child. This sense of being out of sync with one another can escalate as each party becomes more desperate to engage the other, or the relationship may become disengaged as they retreat from each other. These negative interactions create anxiety and alienation rather than fostering coherence and affect regulation.

Interestingly, a number of current psychodynamic treatment approaches also utilize this attachment paradigm. Current research on the neurobiology of attachment builds on a rich psychodynamic tradition of examining psychic development through dyadic interaction (Beebe & Lachmann, 2002). Employing this attachment research, Daniel Siegel has described the intricate communication patterns involved in negotiating connections between parents and children (Siegel & Hartzell, 2003). Siegel highlights not only the formative nature of early attachment relationships but also delineates the ways that parents can repair negative interactions by fostering accurate emotional communication. Similarly, contemporary psychoanalytic theories of psychotherapy focus on the healing power of affective attunement. Intersubjective theories, as described by Buirski and Haglund (2001), focus on the profound human need to be heard and understood. In all of these approaches, there is an emphasis on emotionally meaningful interactions that help us know ourselves and the other. The hallmark of affective attunement, in all of these approaches, is the feeling of clear, emotionally consistent communication. Although it isn't easy to define this type of communication, it does seem to be one of those phenomena that we know when we see it. When my students did a rock-opera parody of the therapy process, the refrain of the therapy client to the therapist was straight from Buirski's intersubjective paradigm "You really get me." When communication works well, we do indeed feel that others really get us.

In applying the attachment paradigm to couples therapy, Sue Johnson (2004, 2002) highlights the fact that attachment needs are lifelong rather than developmental. Noting that feeling grounded in secure, supportive relationships is the cornerstone of adult mental health, Johnson has studied the ways that the therapy process can repair ruptured attachments. As mentioned previously, Johnson moves beyond the singular focus on emotional expression that was common to Satir and Whitaker to analyze the function of human emotional communication. Similar to points made by Watzlawick and other systems theorists, Johnson notes that our communication often obscures rather than clarifies our message. Particularly when we react from a position of insecure attachment, our ability to express what we feel is limited or compromised. While we may be engaged in expressing ourselves, what is often expressed is the defensive surface layer of an experience. By getting underneath the defensive secondary emotions to explore the primary affect in a situation, Johnson makes room for that deeper feeling of being more thoroughly understood.

Although the idea of looking at what is underneath a defensive reaction has been common in many psychological theories, Johnson shows us both the complexity and the efficacy of exposing and reworking emotional miscommunication. Often, a heated argument can give us an entry point to understanding where people begin to misunderstand each other.

Let's go back to the case of Jim and Amy and their argument about planning dinner. If I were to begin a discussion of the argument by asking how they feel, they both would say they feel angry. They are clearly frustrated with each other, and each feels their point is completely valid. At this point, a focus on getting the negative feelings out would be likely to reinforce their defensive, righteous positions. Jim can easily cite examples of times when Amy has been indifferent and unappreciative; Amy feels very strongly that she needs to stand up for herself to feel like a visible adult. Going a bit deeper, we could look at the ways they each feel hurt by the other. There is clearly a great deal of pain in the room, and both Jim and Amy are disappointed by the rejection and invalidation they feel from each other. By going beyond the surface anger and frustration to look at their hurt and disappointment, there is an opportunity to approach each other with care and compassion rather than judgment and disdain.

Facilitating this type of constructive communication is often more difficult than it appears, however, and means applying several of the systems concepts that we have discussed so far. First, the context of the argument must be one of collaboration rather than competition. The therapist needs to make room for both of their viewpoints to help them see how to work together rather than how to win the argument. Second, by employing a circular and multiple-causality approach, the therapist can be curious about all of the factors that contributed to the argument. Like shifting the context of the argument, employing circular causality helps each partner see how they contribute to the pattern, which will feel different from the pattern of blame and defense that they initially use in describing the argument.

Coming from this basic systemic perspective, I can now slow down the communication and understand more about what each partner wanted to express to the other. Similar to what both Satir and Whitaker would have done, we can examine the underlying messages in their communication and try to use the affect to create more authentic connection. Seeing what Jim and Amy were each looking for was the first step in helping them understand each other and express themselves more clearly. Looking at their pattern from an emotionally focused perspective, we see that Jim has felt chronically unappreciated by Amy and has a history of missing the mark when trying to please her. As I help him explore these feelings, we are able to focus on his fear of disappointing her and his very poignant wish to make her happy. We can see that if he could have expressed this desire more directly, she could have tuned in to the intent of his communication. The fact that he wants to feel special and to have her eyes light up when he presents a surprise is so human that it ultimately draws Amy to a more compassionate stance.

At the same time, when we explore Amy's feelings, she is able to express how painful it is to feel invisible to Jim. She is so fearful that he really doesn't care what she wants, and she is longing to feel important to him. When he sees how much it would have meant to her to have him slow down and listen to her request for steak, the tone of the conversation changed. Although the report-level conflict actually became clearer through the discussion (shall we have bruschetta or steak?), the emotionally focused work allowed us to explore and resolve the command-level conflict. The couple was able to see the legitimacy of both Jim's wish to feel special and Amy's wish to feel important and to listen to these needs in a different way. Not coincidentally, from this empathic position, it is much easier to resolve the literal conflict: Whether they decide to have both steak and bruschetta tonight, to take turns, or to do something completely different, the decision will feel different when it comes from a place of each experiencing that their attachment needs are being met.

COMMUNICATION CREATES ATTUNEMENT

The example I've used is from a couples therapy session, and yet I hope that you see the applicability to other forms of therapy. As mentioned in the discussion of intersubjective approaches, these same communication principles are equally relevant in creating the kind of attuned attachment promoting communication between therapist and client. By using miscommunication and relational ruptures as clues to understand unresolved attachment needs, the therapist can both elucidate relational themes and create a deep sense of mutual understanding. One excellent example of this theme is a case study described by Buirski (2005). Buirski is doing a clinical demonstration with a client who has experienced a recent divorce and is clearly in pain, yet seems to be unclear about the process of therapy and the ways that therapy might help. Upon reflection, Buirski notes that the interview demonstrates the difference between a traditional object relations approach to clinical work and a more relational, intersubjective approach to a client.

For the first part of the interview, the therapist is trying to help the client gain insight into the patterns that have led to his problems and to his distress. As Buirski explores the client's history and description of relationships, he becomes internally frustrated with the client's lack of insight and inability to build off the therapist's suggestions. From the therapist's description of his own experience, we know that he is feeling ineffective in working with the client. The client makes a statement that disparages coming to therapy, lamenting that "you have to go see a doctor to help you get interesting?" (Buirski, 2005, pp. 48–49). Buirski responds, "I guess your feeling is then that you're a pretty nice guy but not an interesting one." While the content of the response is neutral, Buirski is aware of his negative internal experience. The client says, "It's sad to say I think you're, uh, I, that's, uh, I think you're right about that." The client experiences Buirski's negative reaction, and Buirski correctly identifies the client's painful feelings in his response. Buirski is touched by the client's openness after his remark. He is more congruent in his communication and the client responds by being more authentic. He shifts the focus to connecting to the client's felt experience and the interview becomes more successful and satisfying. The client also seems more emotionally available and shares deeper and more vulnerable thoughts and feelings.

Buirski provides a transcript of the session, as well as describing the nonverbal aspects of the interchange between him and the client. In addition, he adds his perspective on what he was thinking and feeling during the interview. As mentioned, he uses the case to illustrate the philosophical differences between an interpretive approach and a collaborative approach. Although both object relations theory and intersubjective theory are based on the importance of circular interactions, an intersubjective theorist sees his role as being present and engaged enough with the client to provide an experience of affective attunement.

Again, systems theory provides an explicit language for how to create this type of attuned communication. I would argue that Buirski's communication became more transparent in the exchange just before he switched tactics and remained more effective because it was clearer and more consistent. In the earlier part of the session, his words were communicating that he was curious and interested in the client, but he felt distant and unengaged. The focus on insight and exploration did not seem meaningful to the client, and the positive intent did not translate into a matching impact. Using systems language, the report function of the communication (I want to get to know you) was not matched by the command function (you are someone who is hard to get to know). We can guess that the client is having a similar experience, in that the report function of the communication is that the client is answering questions and participating in his treatment, whereas the command function is that the exchange is unhelpful and confusing. Even as the therapist becomes frustrated, the intent of the communication is to provide help to the client, yet in the beginning of the interview, this intent does not translate into impact. We might also guess that the interpretive approach provided at the beginning of the session felt as though it was geared toward providing insight, as the therapist attempted to explain the reasons for the patient's distress. This approach is not what the client was looking for, but the client's discomfort was communicated only through the lack of connection in the room. When the therapist began to focus on his and the client's subjective experience, the resistance to problem analysis and problem solving ceased.

From a theoretical perspective, the intersubjective therapist would say that clients are always looking for affective connection rather than problem solving, regardless of the report function of their communication. Yet from a systemic perspective, it was the inconsistencies and mixed messages that kept the interview from moving forward in a productive manner. Similarly, when the therapist aligned the implicit and explicit messages of the communication and provided consistency between content and affect, the client experienced the therapist as genuine and began to experience his own story as one that made sense. This required a therapist willing to examine himself from multiple perspectives, rather than claiming and hiding behind the role of doctor. It is often this type of clear, coherent, in-sync communication that both transforms and maintains relationships, as we will see when we explore the concept of change in the next chapter.

In sum, systems theory helps us analyze and transform problematic communication when there is an inconsistency between message sent and message received. It allows us to look at the literal meaning, or report function, of a communication and to see that this meaning is always grounded in the context of relationship variables, or the command function of the message. Moving beyond the explicit and implicit aspects of the message, systems theory helps us understand that there is a difference between the sender's intent and impact and that confusion between these two aspects of communication can be both puzzling and distressing. Finally, communication can have various purposes, from establishing status to solving problems to creating emotional bonds. The ability to create constructive communication is central to productive systems therapy.

CHAPTER 5

Change

I SOMETIMES ASK my students to write down the following statements and then determine which one is correct:

The more things change, the more they stay the same.
You can never step in the same river twice.

Students often do have an opinion about these statements, based on their own experiences with change. Of course, my clever students generally challenge me immediately, noting that choosing one of the statements reflects the kind of either-or perspective that systems thinking is designed to eradicate. I have to agree with them but then can move on to look at the meaning of both statements and the ways that systems thinking relates to each statement. In the first statement, we see change as illusory. Real change is impossible, as there is nothing new under the sun. In the second statement, change is ubiquitous, something we must accept because we can't escape it. Can both statements really be true?

Within systems thinking, not only are both statements accurate, but both statements also reflect a fundamental truth. The first statement helps us see that systems inherently resist change and seek to maintain a certain predictable order. At the same time, systems are constantly reorganizing and transforming themselves. Thus, by design systems have mechanisms for both staying the same and evolving. Further, systems thinking helps us understand the specific conditions that both promote and prevent change. As you will see, I believe that systemic notions of change add immeasurable value to the practice of psychotherapy in a variety of ways.

Why is change such an important concept in psychotherapy? This question may seem so obvious as to be ridiculous, but I think it is worthy of discussion. It brings to mind my favorite therapy joke: How many therapists does it take to change a lightbulb? Only one, but the lightbulb really needs to want to change. While the joke is quite silly, it points to a conflict that is more profound, the existential issue of human control and choice. Do we need to want to change for change to happen, or are we merely the pawns of environmental forces? Is our destiny predetermined by our genes, or our culture, or our early history? Why do we want to change, and how much are we really able to change? What happens when we want the other members of our system to change, but we don't want to change?

Again, while systems theory may not solve these existential dilemmas, I find that it helps me wrestle with these questions in meaningful ways. By resisting change, systems are predictable and reliable. The stability of systems gives us a sense of order and helps create identity. In spite of outside challenges, we can count on our families, our hometowns, or our workplaces to stay at least somewhat constant and immutable. At the same time, we constantly seek improvement and progress. Families evolve to become more functional, businesses grow and become more productive, and children grow and leave home. Or cities fall apart, schools are closed, and countries break apart. All of these changes give us a sense of hope and movement, or serve as cautionary tales that a positive institution must be protected and nurtured, or it can be destroyed.

RESISTING CHANGE: SYSTEM STABILITY

So how do systems change? Interestingly, early systems theorists focused more on how systems stay the same than on how systems change. Early family therapy theorists were heavily influenced by the study of cybernetics, or self-regulating systems. During World War II, the science of cybernetics made huge strides through the work of a number of prominent scientists and mathematicians, including Norbert Wiener (1948). Rather than looking at simple cause and effect, physicists such as Wiener looked at, and then created, systems that used external feedback to provide crucial information on maintaining the system's functioning. Using the concept that systems seek to maintain a steady state of equilibrium, or homeostasis, Wiener examined the processes by which a system can both pursue and then incorporate feedback from the supporting environment or context. The classic example of a self-regulating system is temperature control in modern buildings. A thermostat is set to constantly measure the temperature, or elicit feedback. If the thermostat is connected to a heating system, it will be set to sense the point at which the temperature reaches a particular threshold, and when it does, the heating unit is turned on until the temperature reaches another threshold. When the room is warm enough, the heat turns off. Although the temperature may fluctuate a few degrees, the system is set up to be self-regulating and to maintain a steady state.

Wiener and other scientists used the concept of self-regulating systems to revolutionize all kinds of machines, including developing designs for computers. Although we can't argue that there is a literal, measurable point of equilibrium in most human systems, Bateson and colleagues used these principles of homeostasis and feedback loops to understand the ways that human groups resist change (Bateson, 1972; Nichols & Schwartz, 2001). As in nonorganic systems, Bateson argued that there are rules that establish the types of behaviors that are permitted within a given system. These rules, which are often implicit, serve as a system's thermostat. As we will see later in the chapter, when behaviors begin to exceed certain rules within the system, some type of feedback will occur to keep the behavior in line. Similarly, when not enough behavior is occurring, other feedback will signal the need for more of this behavior.

RULES THAT GOVERN BEHAVIOR

Some of these ideas seem abstract and arbitrary, especially given the fact that the rule governing communication is often out of our conscious awareness. Yet if you begin to examine the types of choices you make in your own context, these ideas typically make sense. I ask my students, "How long can you go without being in touch with your parents before they are worried about you? Similarly, how often would you have to call them for them to become worried about you?" Although these rules are generally not conscious or explicit, students are surprised that they can easily answer the question. In some families, daily phone calls are the norm; in other families a daily phone call would signal that something is wrong. These rules are certainly influenced by culture and by family history, and they may change over time. It is interesting to note the way that the availability of cell phones has changed the expected level of contact for many families. People of my generation often talk about the Sunday evening phone call they made from college, when the long-distance calling rates were especially low. These same friends report that they talk to their own college-age children several times a week. Does this increased level of contact mean that they are closer to their children than they were to their parents? The answer to this question isn't clear, but it is clear that in either instance there are unspoken rules in most systems that tell us how close we should be, how separate we should be, and how both closeness and separation should be maintained. These rules are part of a feedback loop that governs the behavior of the members of the system.

Watzlawick and Bateson were intrigued by the ways that families didn't change, even when confronted by the best intentions of mental health professionals (Watzlawick, Bavelas, & Jackson, 1967; Watzlawick, Weakland, & Fisch, 1974). Probably anyone who works with children has seen the phenomenon of family homeostasis first-hand, when a child whose symptoms have improved in treatment becomes symptomatic again with increased contact with the family. According to the theory, the child's symptoms serve some type of function for the system; therefore, a change in the child's symptoms would threaten the homeostasis. Of course, the vast majority of parents don't want their child to be symptomatic, and this logic can seem counterintuitive at best and pathologizing of parents at worst. And yet a more comprehensive view of homeostasis can reveal the difficulties in removing a child from a family context, teaching the child new skills and strategies, and then returning the child to the original context. The premise of homeostasis explains the pull that the child feels to revert to the previous behavior, even if the family doesn't have a "need" for the symptom.

MODIFICATIONS AND REORGANIZATION

An even more common scenario occurs when a symptomatic child improves, and then another child in the family becomes symptomatic. Again, this scenario is used to validate the principle that a dysfunctional system needs an identified patient, scapegoat or at least the symptomatic behavior to maintain homeostasis. A more careful examination of the theory says less about the pathological need for symptoms and more about the difficult nature of change. In exploring the process of change, systems theorists highlighted the difference between first-order change and second-order change. First-order changes are minor modifications in communication and behavior that allow the fundamental structure and rules of the system to remain the same; second-order change involves a fundamental reorganization of the system (Watzlawick, Weakland, & Fisch, 1974). According to systems theorists, when a child's behavior improves outside the family system, this change is typically a first-order change. In many instances, the original symptom reflects a broader systemic problem that can be addressed only by a second-order change. A recent book reviewing psychotherapy outcome literature calls second-order change "the golden thread that unifies effective treatments" (Fraser & Solovey, 2007, p. 4). In reviewing the outcome literature in anxiety, depression, family therapy, couples therapy, substance abuse, and suicidality, the authors make a compelling case that effective psychotherapy achieves second-order change.

DEEPER LEVELS OF CHANGE

This principle brings to mind a family case that was rich with systemic dynamics and highly resistant to change. The symptom that brought the family to treatment was the 14-year-old daughter's refusal to speak to her father. The parents were in the process of filing for divorce, following the father's disclosure that he had been involved in a long-term affair. The daughter was extremely loyal to her mother and expressed outrage over her father's behavior, while her 12-year-old brother was managing the transition to the divorce by having a good relationship with both parents. The parents were conflicted about how to handle the daughter's reaction, with the mother feeling that the daughter simply needed time to adjust and the father feeling that his daughter's refusal to speak to him was unacceptable. Because the daughter's grades began to drop and she started to display symptoms of depression, the mother was willing to engage in therapy and to look into the daughter's concerns.

In this case, a first-order change would involve addressing the daughter's grades, depression, and difficulty in communicating with her father. If only first order change occurred, she would reluctantly complete her homework, would get out of bed on the weekend, and would have minimal contact with her father. While these problems were addressed with her directly, they were also addressed with each of her parents in order to understand the potential need for second-order change. The daughter's symptoms provided an opportunity to work on key relational dynamics in the system. As the daughter explored her anger toward her father, he was able to listen to her feelings directly and stop seeing them as an extension of her mother's anger. Similarly, the daughter was able to express directly to her mother her concern that her mother could not recover from the divorce, and her mother was able to show that while she was hurt by the father's betrayal, she did not need the protection of her daughter's anger. As the parents were able to build separate relationships with their daughter, they were able to move forward in letting go of each other and of the marriage. Ironically, as they were less embroiled in conflict with one another, they were able to work together more effectively in developing common strategies for helping their daughter with her school work and her mood. Although the theory would have predicted this development, I was still surprised to see that as the daughter seemed ready to end therapy, the 12-year-old brother was arrested for shoplifting!

In this instance, the difference between first- and second-order change was put to the test. If only a first-order change had occurred, the parents may have learned new skills, but the fundamental dynamics and organization of the system would remain the same. The father would have learned that instead of yelling at his son for the shoplifting, he would develop consequences such as requiring the son to earn the money necessary to pay for his legal fees. Similarly, the mother would have addressed the problem behavior rather than ignoring it or chalking it up to normal teenage acting out. But each parent would have maintained the systemic homeostasis by ultimately blaming the other for the son's problem. The mother would have alluded to her belief that if the son had an appropriate male role model, such as a father who did not have affairs, the son would not have been tempted to act dishonestly. Similarly, the father would have complained once again about the mother's indulgence and would have said that he had been telling her for years that her lack of rules and consequences would backfire.

Instead, the parents were able to work together, even as the son complained to each about the other parent. In a strange way, their ability to work together for their son's benefit helped them let go of each other and ultimately moved the divorce along. When their divorce was stalled, they continued to see each other as bad people, but through the process of therapy, they were able to begin to see each other as former partners who were now able to develop a co-parenting relationship for the benefit of their children. We had evidence of a second-order change, as the pattern of the children's symptoms eliciting conflict between the parents was replaced by a more businesslike teamwork between them.

There was a new civility between the parents, and ultimately both children seemed relieved to be able to turn their attention away from their parents' conflict.

Given the positive outcome of this case, we might ask why any system would resist second-order change. Doesn't this story illustrate the fact that homeostasis is a negative force, like psychodynamic resistance, that prevents humans from achieving their potential? Again, the questions are legitimate, but systems theory is especially helpful in highlighting both the constructive and destructive aspects of a system's resistance to change, showing us a healthy skepticism for the potential pitfalls in pursuing change. The reasons that systems resist change are neither random nor arbitrary.

ACCELERATING AND INHIBITING CHANGE

In looking at the potential pitfalls of change, systems theorists examined the specific mechanisms for creating and resisting change. Noting that systems are continuously incorporating messages that help them adapt to their environments, systems theorists labeled messages that tell systems to maintain their course of action *negative feedback* (Watzlawick, Bavelas, & Jackson, 1967). This term has fallen out of favor, largely because the term connotes criticism or complaint, but as used by the original systems theorists, the term was not evaluative and did not have an inherently constructive or destructive connotation. Instead, negative feedback is any message in a system that tells the system to resist change, or change back. Negative feedback tells us to slow down, proceed with caution, and retain the status quo. In our example, the negative feedback would come from one family member trying to reenact the conflictual dynamic between the parents. For example, if the daughter said to her mother, "You know that John would never have done this if Dad had been around more," it represents an enormous shift for the mother to resist the power of the status quo. If the mother accepts the change-back message, she will agree with the daughter and blame the father for the son's problems. It is likely that all family members will experience a strange sort of familiar relief, as the behavior is consistent with the dominant family stories. Mom blames Dad, Dad blames Mom, and whatever we do, we can count on them being upset with each other and having disparaging things to say about one another. This scenario sounds quite unpleasant, but the predictability is in fact comforting. Negative feedback creates stability and consistency in the system. In effect, the system is saying, "This is what we do."

The alternative, of course, is much riskier. Messages that tell the system to keep changing are known as *positive feedback* (Watzlawick, Weakland, & Fisch, 1974), but once again the evaluative connotation is a misnomer. While we as outsiders can point to the significant advantages of change, the process of change is anxiety producing, at best. If Mom and Dad are not fighting, what will they do instead? Will they ever have contact with each other? Will the family completely fall apart? Positive feedback tells the system to continue with the change process, but the outcome of the change is often far from clear.

As framed in this case, the fears that systemic change will lead to a breakdown of the family sound irrational and easy to counteract, but systems theory points out the real danger of second-order change. With a preponderance of positive feedback, systems are prone to change to the point that they are no longer regulated or recognizable. In this case, the second-order change could have looked quite different. The mother could have escalated the argument with the father to the point that she asked for full custody of the son. As she gathered evidence against him and worked to alienate him from his son, the father might have given up and ultimately pulled away. We would see that the positive feedback provided by the parents' actions would create a systemic change, but one that would not be described as positive by most people.

While it may be a family therapy urban legend, I'll never forget a story by a supervisor while I was in training. An outside therapist was doing a live interview and encouraging a family to express their unresolved grief and anger about the mother's earlier disappearance from the family. The therapist had interpreted the son's underachieving behavior as the result of unexpressed anger, and he pushed the family toward second-order change as he encouraged them to directly verbalize their disappointment and anger toward one another. According to the story, after the interview, the son found the family gun and shot his mother. In this instance, the change messages escalated to the point of breaking all of the rules in the system, including prohibitions against violence. Whether or not the story is accurate, the point that change can take on a life of its own and create chaos certainly rings true. Within systems language, this type of escalating positive feedback is known as a *runaway*, which captures the feeling of change being out of control and unregulated. As therapists, we are often called to look for ways to facilitate second-order changes that can bring more fundamental and lasting relief, without putting clients in danger of change that will be disintegrating or disorganizing. The complexity of this task certainly speaks to a less naïvely optimistic view of change.

EVEN AND ABRUPT CHANGE

Another way that systems theory looks at transformation is through the distinction between continuous and discontinuous change. Although the two categories are not always mutually exclusive, these concepts also help capture some of the human experience of change. Continuous change is incremental, linear, cumulative, and gradual; discontinuous change is sudden and transformative. In many biological systems, there often is a complementary process between continuous and discontinuous change, as developmental stages shift, mature, and shift again. In a toddler learning to walk, there is often a period of continuous change, as toddlers learn to practice pulling themselves up and standing on two feet. At some point, however, the child will take off walking, a change that for most parents and toddlers feels discontinuous. As the child practices walking and the family accommodates the child's new skill, another period of continuous change emerges. Again, there are minor modifications in supporting the new stage, but these feel incremental rather than revolutionary.

Systems theorists who focus on the family life cycle, such as Betty Carter and Monica McGoldrick, point out that discontinuous change is indeed more likely around developmental transitions, particularly those that add or lose members of the system (Carter & McGoldrick, 1988). (I'm reminded of my minister's joke about the importance of hatching, matching, and dispatching—many churches' emphasis on birth, marriage, and death are no coincidence, according to systems theory!) McGoldrick starts with a stairstep model of human change, noting that for a time continuous change can feel like being on a plateau (or the run of a stair), which is then followed by a period of discontinuous change, or stepping up to another level (the rise of the stair).

Lynn Hoffman (1981) expanded on this notion of change in what she calls the "spiral platter" model of change. We've all heard the phrase "two steps forward, one step back" to highlight the way that progress is rarely completely linear. Incorporating the metaphor of the spiral, Hoffman notes that an initial move forward, whether experienced as continuous change or discontinuous change, is often followed by a period of retreat or regrouping. If we think about a system's pull toward homeostasis, it makes sense that a change message may be followed by a change back message. After a period of retreat, however, it is often possible for the system to turn the corner and begin the ascent toward more progress. Looking back at the baby learning to walk, it is not uncommon for a toddler to take a few steps and fall, retreat to crawling again, and then finally master the task of walking. In typical physical development, the process does eventually move forward in a fairly linear fashion, but the process of psychological change often becomes bogged down or stuck. Rather than spiraling, often our attempts at change leave us stuck in vicious cycles, feeling that we are walking the same circle again and again.

FINDING THE LOGIC IN RESISTANCE

It is with this sense of psychological stuckness that I have found systemic concepts of change so helpful, particularly strategic approaches. Jay Haley (1963, 1973, 1976, and 1980) and Milton Erickson (Erickson & Haley, 1985) were the originators of strategic therapy. Haley worked first with Bateson and Watzlawick in Palo Alto and then went on to work with Salvador Minuchin in Philadelphia (Nichols & Schwartz, 2001). Haley and Minuchin's ideas are often combined into a single structural-strategic approach, but each takes a distinctive aspect of systems theory as the key foundation to his approach. Haley had a degree in communications, had been in the army, and then came to Palo Alto to work with veterans. Milton Erickson was a psychiatrist who was noted for his creative and often unusual use of hypnosis (Erickson & Haley, 1985), and Haley was heavily influenced by Erickson. As Haley observed the interaction of family members in Bateson's lab, he was intrigued by the implicit rules that seemed to keep people locked in unproductive interactions. While family members certainly didn't intend to drive each other crazy, he noted that there was often an underlying logic to the negative cycles that trapped families. Although no one consciously chose or wanted the symptom that brought the family to treatment, the therapist could see that symptom often served an important function in maintaining the family homeostasis, once the logic of the symptom made sense.

Typical for the systemic approaches of the time, Haley located the cause of human problems in the interactions between family members. Rather than looking at individual pathology or family history, Haley examined the feedback loops that tell family members to behave in ways that keep the problem in place. From the nature of these feedback loops, Haley identified a common pattern known as the solution becoming the problem. In the classic pursuer-distancer pattern, for example, we might see that a wife is starting to feel distant from her husband, and she tells him that she wants to go to the movies over the weekend. The husband has already made plans to attend a baseball game with his friends, and when he tells her about these plans, she becomes angry and talks about how she spends much of the weekend cleaning the house, while he is able to have fun by going to the ballgame. She decides to reorganize all of their closets while he is at the game, and she calls him numerous times to tell of her progress. He is distant on the phone and doesn't seem impressed by her work when he returns home.

The husband responds by staying late at work the next night, telling her that he is also doing his share to contribute to the marriage, but she is even angrier about this distance. She again calls him repeatedly while he is at the office. The more she calls, the later he stays. Soon they have established a pattern in which the more the wife pursues, the more the husband distances, and the more that he distances, the more she pursues. They each have an airtight case to show that their behavior is reasonable, and if the other party would change, everything would be fine. Given the psychodynamic psychotherapy that was practiced as Haley was developing this theory, we can assume that in this case a therapist would want to analyze and ultimately interpret either the husband's fear of intimacy or the wife's need for attention and control. Haley rejected these notions of individual psychopathology, instead saying that in the context of the interactions, these behaviors make sense and don't reflect pathology. For Haley, the interaction was the problem, and the key to change was altering the interaction, not the person.

If the goal is to change the interaction, however, the therapist must be knowledgeable enough about the system dynamic to harness rather than simply confront the system's natural resistance. Again getting away from an individual, pathology-based view, Haley would say that often moving full speed ahead to try to force change only reinforces the problematic feedback loops. In our example, we can see that each partner was trying to create change by increasing the behavior that didn't work, and in doing so, they were caught in feelings of futility and frustration. However, if each partner saw the cycle they were in, rather than seeing their inability to change their partner, the frustration would fade away, and there would be more room for behavioral creativity.

BEYOND REVERSE PSYCHOLOGY

Haley's means of sharing his assessment of the systemic dynamic is known as the positive reframe, and I find it to be an incredibly powerful therapeutic tool. Perhaps in part because of Haley's sarcastic, irreverent tone in writing and in his teaching videos, however, at times Haley's ideas of the positive reframe and the paradoxical injunction are seen as manipulative, coy therapy tricks. Judging the interventions in this way misses the conceptual richness on which they are based, in my opinion. In this instance, the positive reframe might highlight the way that the wife is trying to seek closeness and connection by complaining about the husband's distance, and by calling him repeatedly, she is hoping that he will give her more attention and spend more time with her, because she finds him so funny and interesting. Similarly, the husband's staying late at work is designed to give him more credibility as a good husband and allow him to meet her needs. The hope is that if he works harder and stays away more, she will appreciate him more and be in a better mood when he returns. Unfortunately, the nature of the pattern guarantees that the behavior will only elicit the unwanted reaction from the partner, and the unwanted reaction will increase the already negative cycle.

The positive reframe provides the first step in the change process. When the therapist says, "Of course, you call him every hour at work. You want to show him that you miss him, and you want him to appreciate all that you are doing at home," the husband will be in a better position to think about the problem differently. Suddenly her calls are not about criticism and control; they are about care and connection. Similarly, when the therapist says, "Of course, you need to stay late at work, and the more she calls, the later you will need to stay. You are trying to be productive and get ahead at work to take care of your family. You are staying late at work in order to be a better husband," the wife will also be in position to see the problem differently. Rather than seeing his lateness as a rejection of her, she can see it as an attempt to fulfill the marital contract.

Because the strategic approach relies on behavioral change, the positive reframe is just the first step in setting the stage for change. Haley didn't believe that the reframe provided some type of positive thinking solution that allowed the problem to be better tolerated. Instead, he followed the reframe with a behavioral prescription, which is generally a paradoxical injunction. Haley found a clever way to request that the symptomatic behavior be repeated, which is often called prescribing the symptom. The therapist in this case might say to the wife, "You need to keep calling your husband to show him you care and to feel that you care. I want you to be sure to call him at least five times a day and at least once an hour after you get home from work. You need to let him know that you are thinking of him."

To the husband, the therapist might say, "You need to continue show-ing your devotion to the family by staying late at work. Be sure to watch how much time you spend on the phone and then stay longer, depending on how much time you have been on the phone. You need to show your wife that you are determined to be productive and successful."

The goal of these prescriptions is to set up a therapeutic win–win situation on a couple of different levels. First, if they follow through with the prescription, they will be engaging in the behaviors to please the therapist and to comply with the treatment, not to treat each other badly. The meaning of the behaviors will have to change, and the sense of frustration and futility will no longer cause the pattern to escalate. You can also imagine that the wife's phone calls will be shorter and more pleasant, and given this change, the husband will be less distant when he does finally return home. At the same time, the couple may decide not to follow through with the prescriptions and instead elect to change their behavior. The wife may decide that she is tired of calling her husband, now that she takes it less personally that he isn't coming home. She may use her time to call friends instead and may reverse the pursuer dynamic. Similarly, the husband may not get as much out of staying at work when it doesn't elicit the same disapproval from his wife. He may decide to return home earlier or may respond to his understanding that she wants to be closer by inviting her to the next ballgame. Either way, the therapist has set up a situation in which change is inevitable.

You might be wondering how Haley's approach is different from a simple reverse-psychology procedure, and the distinction is actually important. Certainly, using some of the notions of resistance to change can show us the potential efficacy of reverse psychology. Rather than pursuing change head-on and creating a power struggle, a reverse-psychology perspective employs an almost martial arts sort of accep-tance of our human tendency to be oppositional. If your children won't go to bed at night, take away their bedtime and encourage them to stay up late. In fact, you might want to prohibit them from going to bed at their regular time. The expected outcome is that in time, your children will be begging to go to sleep at their regular time. But as most parents can attest, this strategy can sometimes backfire. And while the ultimate goal of strategic therapy is to change the problematic behavioral cycle, the difference between a simple prescription of the symptom and a more complete strategic intervention is that the therapist's understand-ing of the feedback cycle is the foundation for the specific injunction.

NOT A THERAPY TRICK

Early in my training, I viewed strategic therapy warily, as I felt that there was something unempathic and somewhat deceitful in asking clients to do more of what was already making them miserable. When a 1992 article in the *Journal of Marital and Family Therapy* was devoted to the ethical application of strategic therapy (Solovy & Duncan, 1992), I saw that many of the interventions that I had used were conceptually based on strategic work, although they had none of the tongue-in-cheek tone that seemed to characterize strategic therapy to me. The case that came to mind was one of a 13-year-old girl, Nina, who had recently attempted suicide when she had been grounded by her parents and missed her best friend's slumber party. Initially, I was surprised that Nina was not hospitalized and that the emergency room staff agreed with the parents that family treatment was the best course of action. The parents were very concerned about the events that led to the attempt and felt that the family conflict had been escalating for the past several weeks. They noted that Nina had become moodier, more difficult and increasingly oppositional in the last few months. She had previously been very close to her mother and to her two younger sisters, ages 11 and 8. But since she started the eighth grade, she had stopped letting her younger sister borrow her clothes, had spent more time in her room and less time with the family, and had recently been caught with a cigarette lighter in her pocket. She was angry and sarcastic much of the time, and her parents felt they were losing their daughter.

In the week before the grounding, Nina had told her parents that she and her friends were going to stage a war protest at their small private school. The parents were pleased by this announcement, as it seemed an appropriate use of her adolescent anger. They purchased supplies for making posters and used the event as a chance to talk about politics and history. On the day of the protest, school officials told the students that if they held the protest, they would be suspended. Most of the group, including Nina, continued the protest. They were then taken to the principal's office and suspended from school for the remainder of the week. When Nina's parents came to pick her up, they let her know that she would be grounded for the rest of the week, since she would be missing school all of this time. She felt this punishment was extremely unfair, as her parents had supported her in staging the protest, but her parents were surprised by her lack of judgment in continuing the protest when it was prohibited by school officials. They felt the grounding would help her learn to be more respectful of authority. Nina noted that her friends who were involved in the protest had to pay some type of consequence but were still permitted to attend the slumber party that was scheduled for Friday night. On Saturday morning, while all her friends were still at the slumber party, Nina took a lethal dose of pills. She said she wasn't sure that she wanted to die, but she felt that she couldn't face her friends and said, "I can't live with my parents for another five years!"

FRAMING THE PROBLEM

Although other situational factors were important in this case, the initial positive reframe was easy to provide. Without a hint of irony, I could say to the daughter, "You need to be angry and assertive to get your parents to notice that you are an adolescent and are changing. Unless you get angry and assertive, they will expect you to continue sharing clothes with your sister, listening to school officials without questioning, and being the easy, compliant daughter that you were when you were younger. You aren't going to be able to grow up if that doesn't change." At the same time, I could say to the parents, "Grounding your daughter and fighting with your daughter come from your desire to be involved and show her that you are still her parents. You need to stay involved with your daughter to help her develop better judgment. Without your involvement, she has taken risks that will damage her future, and she needs to see that she can be angry and be separate without being out of control." This positive reframe set the stage for some of the communication and parenting work that followed. Rather than being fearful or resentful of Nina's anger, her parents were able to recognize her bids for greater independence and to stick with the process of setting rules and privileges as they saw that she needed both autonomy and guidance. Similarly, when the parents' restrictions were seen as providing structure rather than as constraining or undermining, we could all look at what kind of structure Nina actually needed. While Nina continued to speak up against her parents' rules, the process was less about whether they would let her grow up and more about helping her develop responsibility and judgment.

ACCEPTANCE AND CHANGE

Given the nature of the reframe, the interventions that followed could also have been seen as paradoxical injunctions, although at the time I would not have described them this way. As we negotiated rules and consequences, I let Nina know that she needed to be angry, speak up, and show her parents that at times they needed to thwart her independence. I now see these types of systemic maneuvers as reflecting a strategic wisdom about the process of change, as I tried to manage the competing needs of stability and transformation. I realize that my underlying attitude moved back and forth between two poles, which in the current literature is described as the tension between acceptance and change. It is beyond the scope of this chapter to do justice to these current ideas, but it is worth noting that the strategic tradition has been carried forward in a variety of contemporary theories.

One of the most notable of these contemporary theories is Andrew Christensen's integrative behavioral couples therapy (Christensen & Jacobson, 2000; Jacobson & Christensen, 1998), which adds an acceptance component to the more traditional behavioral couples therapy popularized and researched by the late Neil Jacobson (Jacobson & Margolin, 1979). Within this approach, couples move back and forth in examining what they need to accept about one another (what can't change) and what they will work to modify (what can change). Of course, for many couples the process of accepting one another reflects a huge change! Other current approaches that take a similar view of the balance between stability and change include Marsha Linehan's DBT (1993) and Stephen Hayes's acceptance and commitment therapy (ACT; Hayes, Strosahl, & Wilson, 1999). In each of these approaches, a great deal of attention is paid to the energy that is wasted and the frustration that is created by trying to change something that is fundamentally immutable. Both approaches borrow from Buddhist philosophy in noting the futility of trying to change or control our emotions (Hayes, Follette, & Linehan, 2004), and the corresponding potential that is released when we can focus on our behaviors, which we can control.

Both DBT and ACT have been applied most frequently with individuals and groups, and in my mind they also show the relevance of incorporating systems theory in working with modalities other than couples and family therapy. These approaches harness the systemic notion that change should not be viewed in a simplistic, linear manner. At times, change may not be possible or desirable, and an understanding of the current situation (positive reframe) may allow clients to relate to the symptom more adaptively rather than trying to remove the symptom. In fact, at times the most productive change that can occur in a system is the relinquishment of change: When a client says, "I am going to stop trying to not be sad and instead accept my sadness," the act of embracing the symptom can derail a counterproductive pattern.

Further, as therapists, we can see that change is a dynamic, circular process that sometimes reflects minor modifications and sometimes reflects an overarching transformation. In either case, the satisfaction of understanding the types of processes that encourage stability and transformation is a huge payoff in applying systemic thinking to clinical work, adding both flexibility and realistic optimism to our work with clients.

In sum, systems theory provides a unique window into the process of human change. Although psychotherapists may equate change with progress and see it as entirely positive, a systems view gives a more balanced, complex view of change. As self-regulating entities, systems use feedback to maintain equilibrium or homeostasis. At the same time, feedback loops also allow systems to transform themselves. Systems use change-inhibiting messages, or negative feedback, to reduce perturbations and maintain homeostasis but also use change-enhancing messages, or positive feedback, to transform themselves. When the change is minor or routine, it is known as first-order change, whereas change that alters the structure of the system is known as second-order change. Change can be gradual and continuous or abrupt and discontinuous. By understanding the fundamental logic of a system, the therapist can take a more sophisticated view of the obstacles to change, which can be useful in creating a positive reframe of the symptom. Based on this positive reframe, the therapist may be able to create a therapeutic win–win situation by prescribing the symptom, a paradoxical injunction. In any event, systems theory helps us understand the dialectic between acceptance and change, which is likely to benefit the therapeutic process.

CHAPTER 6

Structure

MANY YEARS AGO, I attended a weekend retreat sponsored by the agency in which I was doing my postdoctoral fellowship. This agency was experiencing several transitions, including moving from one parent organization to an affiliated parent organization, and as in many mental health organizations, most of the people who worked there felt that they worked too hard for too little money. The uncertainty of the transition compounded some of these concerns, so the agency hosted a retreat to help us determine how to best weather the change. One of the exercises had all of us organize ourselves into groups based on our function and status in the organization. I don't remember the exact directions, but it was something like, "Find the people in the organization who are at your level for the next exercise." I found the other four postdocs, and together we went looking for the administrative and clerical staff, sure that they would want to be in our group. These were the people we hung out with in the evening, after the senior staff had gone home, and commiserated in feeling overworked and underpaid. We were all uncertain about our futures and had a fair amount of anxiety about the impact of the upcoming changes in the organization. I can still remember feeling shocked that the staff members refused to be part of our group. They were not completely surprised to hear that the postdocs believed we occupied the same status that they did in the organization, but their experience was completely different. I was humbled to hear how much privilege I had as a clinical staff member with a doctoral degree, in comparison with the person who had to make the coffee and answer the phones. Even before the actual exercise began, the task of consciously identifying the subsystems within the agency was illuminating.

INVISIBLE LEVELS AND POSITIONS

Most systems have an invisible but identifiable structure that establishes some type of hierarchy and role differentiation and is made up of subsystems that then constitute the larger system. In the last chapter, we saw that systems are governed by rules that help them maintain consistency and identity and also navigate change. In a related manner, this chapter looks at the ways that systems are structured and organized. This structural approach is often used in conjunction with the strategic approach we explored in the last chapter, as the rules that maintain homeostasis are certainly part of what determines a system's structure. But structural theory goes beyond strategic therapy in examining the hierarchy, roles, and boundaries that give the system a form so that it can function.

SUBSYSTEMS

As we saw when we looked at context, systems are made up of parts, or subsystems, that then make up larger wholes. This relationship between parts and wholes is both simple and profound and particularly important in looking at system structure. In the 1950s, the writer Arthur Koestler (1979) coined the term *holon* (p. 33) to label distinct subsystems that are part of larger systems. This term was designed to capture the important systems notion that most objects are simultaneously parts and whole and that examining whether we are considering an object a part or a whole at any given moment will help us understand a phenomenon more accurately. The term is somewhat awkward and is rarely used today, but I find that the concept continues to have utility. In looking at my work example, we see that the postdocs believed that there was a junior-staff holon, which was comprised of the postdoc holon and the support staff holon. If we were to graph the structure of the agency, we could see that the junior-staff holon shared some functions in the agency (working in the evening, answering telephones), yet the postdoc holon also had more status by virtue of sharing certain functions with the senior-staff holon (seeing clients, writing articles for the agency newsletter). This example shows that while the idea of structure in a system may seem obvious, the simple exercise of identifying subsystems can be useful. Further, the shift between parts and wholes can help us identify what is and isn't working in a system.

Within family therapy, the originator of structural therapy is Salvador Minuchin, one of the few family therapy pioneers who is practicing today (Minuchin & Fishman, 1981). Minuchin was trained as a physician, worked with Nathan Ackerman in New York, went to Israel to work with displaced children in 1952, and then returned to the United States in 1954 to begin psychoanalytic training at the William Alanson White Institute, which utilized the interpersonal theory of Harry Stack Sullivan. In 1962, he visited Palo Alto and began his friendship and collaboration with Jay Haley (Nichols, 2010). He later worked with Haley in Philadelphia, so the complementary nature of the structural and strategic approaches is no accident. Minuchin's basic premise is both simple and profound—that when there is a problem in a system, it signals a dysfunction in the structure of that system. By first understanding and then realigning the structure of the system, the problem can be resolved.

UNIVERSAL FAMILY STRUCTURES?

While Minuchin's premise is simple, it is not without controversy. Minuchin has been criticized for suggesting that there are universal family structures that create health and others that create dysfunction. The belief that there is a correct structure for families (one that is universally functional) and an incorrect structure for families (one that is universally dysfunctional) seems to fly in the face of the both-and thinking that is common to systems approaches. The implication of the theory, for example, is that parents should have more power than grandparents in raising children. Yet, there is a wide range of beliefs across cultures about the acceptable level of involvement for grandparents, and these cultural differences are not addressed in the theory. In addition, the theory places a good deal of emphasis on hierarchy. A clear, unambiguous hierarchy is seen as a sign of system health. In the 1980s, however, feminist family therapists began challenging ideas around the functionality of hierarchy. At this point in time, the term *feminist* has become so loaded that I am hesitant to use it without a great deal of explanation. Yet the tension between the newly established family therapy order, particularly as represented by Minuchin's structural theory, and the feminist family therapy movement ultimately lead to a dialogue that can help us understand hierarchy and power in a more realistic, comprehensive manner.

THE PROBLEM WITH HIERARCHY

In working with families, one of Minuchin's classic prescriptions was to reduce the involvement of the mother and increase the involvement of the father. In doing so, Minuchin would challenge mothers to create a stronger generational boundary between themselves and their children and to allow fathers a greater voice in the parenting process. Feminist family therapists noted that these prescriptions didn't take into account the cultural context of this family dynamic and frequently pathologized a mother's investment in her children, which has a long tradition in a variety of psychological theories. How do we know how much a mother should be involved with her children? When a father feels uninvolved with his family, how do we know that the mother has kept him at a distance? Walters, Carter, Papp, and Silverstein (1988) wrote extensively about our assumptions that close relationships cause psychopathology and looked at the lack of evidence for these theories. These theorists rightly question the underlying values of the therapist, which are frequently unexamined and can be unconsciously imposed on the client. As a middle-class American therapist, I may have beliefs that a mother who wants to remain close to her children during their adolescence does so because she has unresolved dependency needs. Walters and colleagues question the cultural assumptions that overvalue independence and autonomy and pathologize connection and closeness.

As we have already seen, even more than challenging the question of a mother's involvement with her children, the feminist movement of the 1970s and 1980s took the family therapy establishment to task for colluding with the problem of domestic violence (Goldner, Penn, Sheinberg, & Walker, 1990). As we have discussed in looking at multiple and circular causality, one grave problem of blindly applying systems theory to intimate violence is that it can be used to blame the victim of violence. A look at structural theory takes these concerns one step further to note the problems inherent in a patriarchal society. What are the consequences of a hierarchical structure? Who determines how power is distributed in a system? How do economic and political power translate into what happens in families?

Using these questions, feminist psychologists have worked to raise awareness of the invisible power structures in our culture and in families and have often taken the perspective that psychological change must include social change. Early on, attempts were made to create more egalitarian power structures, both in the therapy room and in treatment agencies. From this perspective, we could say that power often corrupts and is used to suppress and stifle marginalized voices. An acceptance of current power structures gives unfair advantage to those at the top, whether the head of a corporation or the head of a family. Those at the bottom of the hierarchy are expected to accept the authority of those at the top, and in submitting to authority, they are often exploited. Because this patriarchal system has been in place so long, it is easy to accept it as a natural social order, and it is difficult to see the costs and consequences of such a system. However, the symptoms of an exploitive, dominance-based hierarchical system are easy to see, whether you look at child abuse, domestic violence, or corporate fraud and theft.

While no one would argue the virtues of child abuse, a structural perspective would argue that hierarchy is not only *not* evil but also necessary in healthy systems. From this perspective, authority limits chaos and provides safety. Rather than oppressing those at the bottom of the hierarchy, an appropriate structure provides clarity and improves functioning. Whether we are talking about workers or children, in this paradigm people feel more secure when they know their role and when the parameters around that role are clear. So how do we resolve the conflict between these two perspectives?

EMPOWERMENT VERSUS DOMINATION

One answer to the conflict lies in the concept of power. The initial social justice concept of power implies dominance, coercion, and force. In exploring this concept, Rampage (2002) labeled it *power over.* This power involves an unquestioning acceptance of authority, a type of "do it because I said so" mentality. In contrast, *power to* includes having the authority and agency to get things done. This type of power involves efficacy and competence but does not utilize force or domination. Although this concept of empowerment may seem to fit best in egalitarian power structures, it can also be applied to hierarchical structures and helps explain why some hierarchical structures work well. If we look back at my work retreat, we see that everyone in the system was feeling overworked and wanted more acknowledgment. The postdocs complained that we felt exploited because we completed many hours of clinical service for less reward than the senior staff, and our future with the agency and in the field was uncertain. The staff complained that they were asked to do all kinds of menial jobs that seemed invisible and unimportant, and most also wanted their job to have a career path. In both instances, a *power over* mentality suggests one of two solutions. In accepting the *power over* structure, we stick with the premise that what we were asked to do was in our job descriptions and that we should accept our position and quit complaining. Rejecting the *power over* mentality suggests that the agency was inappropriately exploiting the workers at the bottom of the hierarchy and should try to create a more egalitarian structure. We would share responsibilities for making coffee, we would rotate evening hours, and we would create a more collaborative system for making decisions, including a greater voice for the postdocs and the staff members.

Although we didn't use this language at the time, I think the consultant who facilitated the retreat helped us examine our structure from a *power to* perspective. As we explored our various subgroups and looked at our complaints, a number of minor changes were implemented that helped all of us feel more empowered in our jobs. The senior staff was both surprised and ultimately grateful for all of the clerical staff's efforts to keep things moving forward, and they used this realization to be more explicit in both requesting tasks and acknowledging the work that was being done. The senior staff also devoted time to career counseling and planning for the postdocs, so that our efforts felt like a step in a professional trajectory rather than cheap labor. It is interesting to me that these *power to* interventions simultaneously helped us accept the power structure as they reinforced our roles in the system, and yet they modified the power structure because we were listened to and felt less invisible. As we will see when we talk about therapeutic interventions, this combination of both maintaining and modifying a structure is a common theme.

COLLABORATION AND COMPETITION

In the abstract, the idea of using an empowerment model is almost universally appealing, yet when conflict exists in relationships, it can be difficult to implement. Both Bateson (1972) and Watzlawick (Watzlawick, Bavelas, & Jackson, 1967) categorized patterns of conflict in relationships according to complementary and symmetrical interactions. In a complementary interaction, one type of behavior (e.g., dominance) elicits the opposite behavior from the other (e.g., submission), whereas in symmetrical interactions, a behavior (e.g., boasting) elicits a similar behavior (e.g., counter boasting) from the other. Expanding on the notion of circular causality, Watzlawick described the ways that complementary interactions can be self-reinforcing and can sometimes be polarizing. It is easy to picture interactions in which dominance is met with submission, which then reinforces and ultimately increases the dominance, and this in turn creates even more submission. These complementary patterns can lead to role rigidity and inhibit conflict resolution.

When I witness complementary patterns that seem entrenched, I have found it helpful to look at the difference between collaboration and competition. When conflict is addressed competitively, there will be a winning side and a losing side, and the loser is obliged to accept the wishes of the winner. In contrast, a collaborative perspective requires the conflict to be resolved to the satisfaction of both sides, at least in theory creating the classic win–win situation (Fisher & Ury, 1991). It is naïve to believe that all conflict can be solved collaboratively, and critics of this model note that resolving conflict collaboratively is almost always more time and energy intensive than more unilateral methods. Yet I have found the concept of collaborative conflict resolution to be one of the most powerful I have used in therapy. Similar to our discussion of moving from either-or to both-and perspectives, the idea of collaborative conflict resolution rests on the idea that within a close relationship, a competitive approach will inherently set up a power-over experience that will engender resentment. To paraphrase one of my favorite couple therapists, Frank Pittman, you can't be happily married and right at the same time (Pittman, 1989). Part of human nature is that it feels great to be right, and yet Pittman's statement illuminates an important truth: In most cases, if our partners feel they are wrong, it hurts the relationship, and there is no way to hurt the relationship without hurting the self. I have found that using this collaborative paradigm is extremely helpful in implementing a power-to approach, as it clarifies that sharing power is effective in the long run. Without this foundational perspective, sharing power looks like an act of generosity, and accepting the will of the other can feel like martyrdom. Although collaboration does not have to imply equality, collaborative conflict resolution does have a quality of fairness and respect that is not present in power-over approaches.

POWER AND PRIVILEGE

Of course, there are many human systems that are neither equal nor fair. When we discuss a hierarchical structure, there is no way around the fact that those at the top of the hierarchy have more power and privilege. Understandably, a discussion of privilege is likely to make most of us uncomfortable. We want privilege, and yet in many situations, our privilege comes at the expense of someone else, so both wanting and having privilege can make us feel guilty. Yet I would argue that a discussion of privilege is essential to elucidating the power structure of most systems and that understanding this structure can enable us to create more equitable, functional systems. One of my favorite metaphors for privilege comes from Peggy McIntosh (1988), who likens privilege to an invisible backpack that we all carry with us. The elements of privilege at our disposal are like items in the backpack in that they serve as resources at crucial moments. She notes that the backpack is invisible because most of us are unaware of our privilege, and like items in a backpack, we are most aware of what we don't have when we need it. It can be painful yet illuminating to become aware of the resources at our disposal when it highlights the fact that others do not have these resources.

During that same postdoc year, I was seeing clients in a community center and was frustrated when one of my clients could not receive her medical benefits. We located a paperwork problem, and I coached her in how to take the paperwork to the agency to fix the problem. She spent a morning waiting for her turn to speak with someone, only to be told that the problem could not be fixed and that she was not eligible for benefits. When she told me about the situation, I immediately picked up the phone and called the office, saying, "This is Dr. Smith-Acuña, and I need to speak with a supervisor." I continued up the chain of command, asking for each person's supervisor, until I found the person who could correct the problem. I tried to teach my client the skills of being appropriately assertive and persistent in asking for help, but I'll never know how much the privilege of my title and my race actually solved the problem.

Even outside the professional arena, issues of power and privilege are both ubiquitous and often invisible. When my daughter was in seventh grade, her school offered a special prize as an incentive to sell items for a fund-raiser. Students who sold a certain amount were taken to a recreation center by a double-decker bus for an afternoon of pizza and bowling. She qualified for the trip, and when we asked which other students had received the prize, we were uncomfortable to learn that all of the other winners were middle-class white students, even though the school had lots of racial, ethnic, and socioeconomic diversity. My daughter countered our discomfort by saying, "All of the kids had the same opportunity to earn these prizes. Anyone could have gone door-to-door to sell the wrapping paper." As is typical with invisible privilege, my daughter had no awareness that she had earned her prize by calling a few relatives and that having to go door-to-door in a poor neighborhood put her classmates at a disadvantage.

THE THERAPIST'S POSITION

Luckily, this greater understanding of power and privilege is consistent with a systemic view of structural theory. Returning to Minuchin's work, we can often translate these ideas of power and privilege into the ideas of status and hierarchy that he addresses in therapy (Minuchin & Fishman, 1981). One of my favorite examples comes from a live interview that he did at a conference in Chicago (Minuchin, 1997). He was starting an interview with a family in which the 14-year-old son had been aggressive and rageful, to the point of hitting his mother on more than one occasion. He stood in front of the son, held up his hand, and then asked the son to punch his hand. The son made a fist and hit Minuchin's palm. Minuchin nodded his head thoughtfully and said, "That's not bad, but I think you can hit harder." The son hit him again, and this time Minuchin said, "That's pretty good. You can hit pretty hard for a 14-year-old." As is true of Minuchin's best work, this intervention establishes structure and empowers people within that structure. We could say that he is showing the boy who is boss because he is not hurt by the blow and even asks to be hit harder. At the same time, he compliments the boy on his strength. Discussing the intervention later, he noted that the boy needs to feel strong and powerful in appropriate ways, not through hitting his mother or believing that he is stronger than the adults around him.

HEALTHY AND UNHEALTHY BOUNDARIES

With an awareness of issues of power and privilege, we can look at the specific concepts that are associated with structural theory. One of the most useful concepts is boundaries. The term *boundary* has become part of our popular vernacular, as in "She has no boundaries!" But what do we really mean when we say a person has no boundaries? Boundaries are designed to define a space and determine what can enter and leave the space. Using the analogy of a cell membrane, we can see that boundaries need to have enough structure to contain what is inside but be permeable enough to allow substances to enter and exit the cell as needed. When we think of human social systems, the substance that generally enters and leaves the system is information, both verbal and nonverbal. Boundaries can be thought of as the rules that govern the amount and type of information that can enter and leave a system and therefore help regulate the amount of closeness and proximity we experience in relationships. Someone with poor boundaries will leak information inappropriately; someone with rigid boundaries is overly closed and doesn't share enough information to be close or connected.

We can describe boundaries around people, but the concept of boundaries is also helpful in defining and describing systems and subsystems. Early in the development of family therapy theory, attempts were made to categorize systems according to their structure and, in particular, their boundaries. In general, problematic systems were thought to be enmeshed or disengaged. Enmeshed relationships involve a high level of connection with lots of shared information but not enough structure between the individual members. Boundaries around enmeshed families were thought to be rigid, as the space between family members was fluid and connected, but outsiders were kept out. In contrast, disengaged families were thought to have rigid internal boundaries, which created both distance and separation between members but allowed more connection to the outside world. Certain presenting problems were considered more likely to occur in enmeshed systems, and others would be more common in disengaged systems. In reality, it is frequently difficult to characterize entire systems as enmeshed or disengaged. Further, the quality of these boundaries tends to change over time. Regardless of this difficulty with classification, however, the idea that relationships can have enmeshed or disengaged qualities, based on the nature of the boundaries between people, is quite helpful. When a relationship feels overly entangled, with an unclear sense of where one person ends and the other begins, interventions designed to strengthen boundaries and create a greater sense of individuality are likely to be helpful. Similarly, when relationships feel cold, distant, and uninvolved, interventions that relax boundaries and create more connection are generally worthwhile.

Boundaries around subsystems are often used to define and establish hierarchical structure. Family therapists are especially concerned with generational boundaries, but looking at the boundaries between and within various levels of any organization is often beneficial. Structural therapists pay special attention to the parental subsystem and the way it performs executive functions. This subsystem exists whether or not the parents are together as a couple; however, rules and boundaries are somewhat different if the parents are no longer together. Boundaries around this subsystem should be clear and distinct enough for children to know that their parents have a separate relationship that exists to provide for them but is not under their control. Boundaries around the subsystem should also be permeable and fluid enough for children to feel that they are valued and important. Regarding the family hierarchy, when boundaries are overly loose, there is a quality that parents are not in charge, which may result in the relationship feeling more like a friendship than a parent–child relationship.

Even in systems other than families, boundaries within a particular hierarchical level are expected to be looser than those between levels. If we picture this visually, without adequate boundaries between levels, the hierarchy will loosen and slip. I'm reminded of faculty colleagues who have become too close with students and blurred the boundaries by talking with students about confidential faculty business, such as student and faculty evaluations. In these instances, the students who are privy to the leaked information often feel a special sense of status, yet in most of these cases, the boundary violation creates other problems in the system. Students become confused by the conflict in the communication, and due to their student role they may lack the ability to put the information in perspective, and may then feel alienated from other faculty members. In the most extreme cases, this type of boundary violation can set up a pathological triangle in which the faculty member and the aligned students get connected at the expense of other faculty members or students.

Similarly, many systems thinkers, Haley (1980) in particular, note that double-bind communication is most problematic when it includes a generational boundary violation. While graduate students may or may not be in a different generation, Haley's concept is equally applicable to other hierarchical boundaries. In one instance, a group of students reported the bind they felt when a faculty member commented on what he believed was unethical behavior on the part of another faculty member. He did not address the problem directly, stating that the problem had no solution, and yet he mentioned that they could go to university personnel with the problem. Although they felt honored that the faculty member had shared this information with them, there was a mixed message about the most adaptive way to handle the information (there is no point in addressing this problem, but the responsible thing to do is to report the problem), and the implicit message was that discussing the problem was against the rules of the system. Of course, the fact that the rest of the faculty eventually learned about the problem indicates that the double bind was eventually addressed, but what I found most helpful in this case was understanding the level of distress caused by the boundary violation.

This example of boundary violations within a system also brings up another important concept in structural theory, that of roles. Within most systems, members play different roles to accomplish the task of the system. To be adaptive, roles should be clear and defined but not rigid. Roles can be formal and explicit, such as the difference between faculty members and students, and they can be informal and implicit, such as peacemaker and troublemaker roles. Often one of the signs of dysfunction in a system is that roles are so rigid that they don't allow members to express their individuality. Conversely, unclear roles create confusion and anxiety. Family therapists labeled different roles that tend to be problematic, such as the parentified child, the identified patient, and the scapegoat. But other roles, such as the savior and the mascot, can be equally problematic if they become too rigid and don't encourage both individual and systemic growth and change.

Armed with background knowledge of power, collaboration, privilege, rules, roles, and boundaries, we can return to the work of the structural therapist. The goal of the therapy, broadly speaking, is to identify the problems in the structure and facilitate the realignment of the structure. When I think of this work, I often see a giant Calder mobile that for some reason isn't hanging in balance. I don't know initially if some pieces are too heavy or large or some are too small, if some are too close together or too far apart, or if there needs to be more space between the various levels of the mobile. But my first task is to see the system in action, so I can identify the problems in the structure.

OBSERVING THE STRUCTURE

The initial step in identifying the problem is to join with the system so that the therapist gets an accurate and authentic picture of the interactions that maintain the problem. When structural therapists talk about joining, they are referring to something similar to the type of alliance building that is common in most therapy, yet there is more to joining than building an alliance (Minuchin & Fishman, 1981; Minuchin, 1974). What I find especially useful about structural approaches is the sophistication involved in positioning relationships in the system. That positioning starts right from the beginning, as the therapist positions herself as someone who is both helpful and challenging to the entire system.

The typical steps described in joining are taking the time to hear from every member of the system and showing some appreciation for the perspective of each person. Unlike the experiential approaches we discussed, however, the point isn't necessarily to make room for the expression of thoughts and feelings; instead, it is to set the stage for the family to enact the structure in the room and to clearly exhibit the problematic structure through the enactment. The therapist looks for clues about system structure in behaviors such as where people sit, how much they talk, and with whom they make eye contact. As the therapist is joining the system, she is trying to position herself as an ally to each member of the system and, through her questions and observations, also as an ally to the system as a whole. Through these interventions the therapist becomes a part of the system, which reduces the homeostatic reaction that will occur if she is experienced as an outsider. My colleague Michael Karson calls this type of joining "finding a place to stand" (2010).

Next, through questions and tasks, the therapist moves from joining the system to creating an enactment. This term sounds very official and stage like, but any good therapy creates an enactment. Rather than simply describing the problem in a detached, experience-distant manner, therapy typically involves allowing the client to create the problem in the room and then showing the pattern to the client directly. When everyone in the room has actually experienced the dynamic in action, the therapist can move to the next stage of intervention, repositioning the structure of the system. Repositioning is generally done through some type of behavioral prescription, but this type of intervention has a different feeling than a straightforward behavioral exercise. There is a more dramatic feeling to running through the family script, then stopping the action and offering a different outcome. The novel outcome generally involves people treating each other in new ways, and again the goal of treating each other differently is to change rules, roles, or boundaries, which will alter a system's structure.

One excellent example of a structural intervention can be seen in a family therapy training tape done by Braulio Montalvo at the Philadelphia Child Guidance Center in the early 1970s (Minuchin, 1974). The case involves an African American single mother and her four children, who range in age from 10 to 4. The presenting problem is that the second oldest child was playing with matches from her older brother's chemistry set and accidentally lit a mattress on fire. The brother was caring for his three younger sisters and heroically took the mattress to the bathtub and extinguished the fire before calling his mother at work. As Montalvo moves about the room and talks with each family member, we see that the oldest child is in a parentified role, is extremely responsible, and talks for the other children. The second daughter is in the identified patient role, as the family is organized around all of the things that she does wrong. Rather than paying attention in the session, she pulls out one of her schoolbooks, and her mother very critically admonishes her to pay attention. Montalvo uses that moment to create an enactment, as he instructs the mother to get the daughter to read aloud. The mother is dismissive of her daughter's skill, and Montalvo uses the enactment to set the stage for repositioning: He says to the mother, "What is going on with you? She is reading very well. You must be doing something right as her mother." This simple intervention highlights the mother's behavior in keeping her daughter in the identified patient role and simultaneously strengthens her role as the mother.

Montalvo goes on to give the behavioral prescription, which is for mother to spend 5 minutes each day teaching the daughter to light matches safely. This intervention clearly has strategic underpinnings, as the symptom (lighting matches) is being reframed as a skill to be mastered and is prescribed rather than prohibited. In assigning the mother to work with the identified patient, he also removes the parentified child from the place of authority and gives both the mother and the daughter a chance to be successful. There is a poignant beginning to the second session with this family, as we learn that the mother and daughter practiced lighting matches not once, but twice each day! The intervention gave the mother an achievable way to inhabit the maternal role, and gave the daughter a more adaptive way to seek and accept attention.

THE STROKE AND THE KICK

A simple description of structural therapy interventions is that the therapists must give every family member a stroke and a kick. We can certainly see the stroke and the kick in the intervention with the mother, as he says, "What is going on with you?" paired with "You must be doing something right as her mother." Although the terminology is too authoritarian for my taste, I have found the stroke and kick concept to be extremely useful in therapy, with individuals as well as with couples and families. More than many therapy approaches, I think that structural theory shows us that true empowerment involves owning our strengths and simultaneously addressing our weaknesses. To use different language, this systemic balancing act of realigning dysfunctional structures combines active support with direct interpretations. This combination can be easily misused when the therapist does not recognize issues of power and privilege, and yet it can be helpful when it is employed collaboratively.

STRUCTURE IN WORK SYSTEMS

I'm reminded again of the case of Carol from Chapter 3, who was learning to be more effective with her adolescent daughter. Interestingly, Carol was also having trouble with her employer. Carol was an administrative assistant in a public relations firm, and she had taken on a project under one of the firm's directors, Ellen. She experienced Ellen as distant, harsh, and demanding and was beginning to dread going to work. Carol felt put down by her boss's questions and requests, and from her descriptions in session, it appeared that she responded to Ellen in an anxious, apologetic manner. Although being on the project could have represented an acknowledgment of Carol's previous good work, she described working under Ellen as a curse that she had hoped to avoid in the firm. She was worried that the only way out of her misery was to find another job.

Looking at Carol's problem structurally, we see that she experienced herself as being in the role of ineffective, incompetent subordinate. She resented the feeling of being put down and unappreciated but didn't know how to restructure her role and find more power in the system. As we explored her discomfort, Carol noticed that some of her peers resented working with Ellen and tried to avoid her, yet other women in her firm worked well with Ellen. Using a structural perspective, I was able to help Carol identify room for movement in the system. Instead of using her colleagues to complain about Ellen's demeaning behavior, Carol began to look at her own behavior and the behavior of her peers to understand how to improve her position in the system. She noticed that when Ellen was assigning her tasks, she was anxious and found it hard to get a clear picture of what Ellen wanted. Because she didn't understand what Ellen was requesting, she made more mistakes than usual, and Ellen was impatient and critical of Carol's mistakes. Carol would respond with apologies and promises to do better, sometimes even crying as she apologized, but later she would be angry with herself for appearing so weak and deferential, qualities that she believed made Ellen judge her even more harshly.

While I was empathic with how painful it was to be criticized by Ellen, I also confronted Carol to help her see that her deferential behavior and her anxiety were perpetuating the problem. You might see my empathy as the stroke in structural theory and my confrontation as the kick; the combination of these two perspectives helped Carol feel less angry and judgmental toward herself and more ready to actively address her situation. Carol could have put a great deal of energy into complaining to coworkers about Ellen, which could easily have set up a pathological triangle within the system. She could have been comforted by the knowledge that some of her coworkers dreaded working with Ellen, and their joint complaints could have created a kind of pseudo closeness that would have diverted Carol from her negative feelings about herself.

I believe that this type of triangle could also have occurred in therapy if I had simply validated Carol's negative feelings about Ellen without looking at her role in maintaining the problem. Instead, Carol looked for ways to feel stronger and more competent within the system. She noted that she had enjoyed working with someone else in the company, Theresa, who had recently been promoted. She invited Theresa to lunch and asked for advice about how to run projects more efficiently. As we discussed how she received information from Theresa, it became clear that she needed to do more preparation before her meetings with Ellen and that she could end meetings with Ellen with a review of her plan of action so that she could be sure that she understood Ellen's instructions. As Carol took more initiative in improving her work skills, she felt less anxious and made fewer mistakes. She had a clearer sense of how to accept Ellen's authority without feeling demeaned, and Ellen was more respectful as Carol was more engaged and assertive. Carol continued to experience Ellen as overly critical but was able to finish the project successfully and did not have to leave her job. In the end, she was invited to join Theresa in a different department in the company, and her job satisfaction improved dramatically.

You might say that the therapy was helpful to Carol because it provided a supportive environment in which to explore her painful feelings without fear of the judgment or criticism she experienced at work. Alternately, you might say that through my questions and observations, I provided assertiveness training and taught Carol communication skills so that she was effective in dealing with Ellen. While I think that there is truth in both of these perspectives, I believe that understanding the structural elements of Carol's situation made both of these interventions more potent. Carol's work system was problematic because the power structure allowed Ellen to be overly dominating, and Carol's personal characteristics reinforced this pattern. By recognizing the structural challenges in the system, we could identify the dysfunctional role that Carol was playing (incompetent, apologetic assistant) and the boundary problems that reinforce this role (that she was too afraid to ask questions and get enough information to get her job done effectively). The rules of the system allowed Carol to do things like invite Theresa for lunch to get more mentoring. Further, the roles were not rigid enough to prevent the problem from improving. As Carol's work performance improved, Ellen became more respectful, and the communication was better on all sides. The project was completed successfully, adding to Carol's sense of competence and efficacy. Although her position of assistant did not change, one could argue that her success improved her status in the system.

Did Carol's individual work of becoming less anxious and more competent actually change the system? It isn't easy to answer this question as an individual therapist, but I believe that these changes often do ripple throughout an organization. In Carol's case, a bad outcome could have reinforced a culture of anxiety, poor performance, and unhealthy criticism. Without the changes that we described, people within the system might believe the idea that Ellen is impossible to please and that she runs off good employees. For Carol, a continuation of the original dynamic could have validated her fear that she can't function as an adult in the real world. Fortunately, this more balanced and three-dimensional view of the system allowed Carol to change her behavior, and in turn, the system functioned more effectively.

Systems theory offers a unique perspective on organizational structures. Systems can be understood through the ways that their subsystems are organized hierarchically. In turn, hierarchies are maintained by boundaries, which ideally are distinct but permeable. Position within a system is also determined by the roles of system members, which at best are clear but not rigid. Challenges to the structural therapy model have allowed a more in-depth exploration of issues of power and privilege, which are often the product of hierarchical structures.

In this chapter, we focused on the ways that systems are organized and on the interactions between people that create and maintain this organization. Although systems theory looks at a variety of levels of human experience, we see that the internal world of system members can also help us understand and intervene with systems. The interplay between individual and group histories over time is explored in more depth in the next chapter.

CHAPTER 7

History and Development

TWO NIGHTS BEFORE I began writing this chapter, I had an especially vivid dream. I was my same, middle-aged self, but I was in my high school boyfriend's kitchen, talking with his mother. We were discussing the difficulties she would face in getting her three children to school in the fall, particularly now that her son, my boyfriend, would be attending college. As often happens in dreams, there was no real logic to the fact that I was still dating my high school boyfriend and that in the dream we were getting ready to break up because of this college transition. I was initiating the breakup, and it seemed that his mother also approved of our ending the relationship. My high school best friend came by to tell me that I shouldn't worry about my boyfriend; he would be attending an excellent local art program, and he would be fine. Although I felt some sadness at the breakup, I was reassured by my friend's words, and I wondered if I would need to see my boyfriend to say good-bye, or if he was already finished with me. I woke up before he appeared in the dream.

It is a risky business to ask a reader who is probably a mental health professional to read about a dream, and I am guessing that you have probably already started to interpret the dream. Before you do, however, I should let you know that I had the dream just a few days before my daughter's boyfriend was leaving for college. How much does this information change your interpretation of my dream? What does the dream have to do with the system, and what does the system have to do with the dream?

PREDICTABLE DEVELOPMENTAL CHANGE

The timing of my dream illustrates one of the key concepts shared by systems theory and by psychodynamic theories, the centrality of developmental level on human experience. Many traditional dynamic theories look at the primacy of early development, with an emphasis on the stages that are shaped by our biological development. Before having children, I wondered about Freud's early preoccupation with different erogenous zones, which seemed overly narrow and deterministic. Further, the idea that the key foundation of our personality could be set by the age of 5, hopefully with the resolution of the Oedipal complex (Freud, 1909; Freud and Strachey, 1962), seemed to minimize the human capacity for change. Yet a closer study of the psychodynamic view of change is consistent with the systems view that we have discussed already, highlighting the tension between stability and transformation. Developmental theories show us that each stage is built on the stage before it, that what happens in the past influences but does not determine our struggles in the present. Further, developmental theories tend to combine both continuous and discontinuous change. We see that periods of incremental change, when a developmental stage is mastered, are often interspersed with periods of more abrupt change, when we take on a new level or stage.

A developmental perspective tends to have a great deal of descriptive value. If you could know only one thing about a person and wanted to guess at her experience, knowing her developmental level would almost certainly give you important information, regardless of other contextual variables. Knowing that I am a middle-aged woman will probably bring certain assumptions to mind about the themes and issues that I am addressing in life. A systems view of human development adds the context of the broader system and tends to focus on key elements of the family life cycle. This approach tends to make the couple the central unit and to follow the developmental trajectory through joining two families by marriage, having children, raising children, facing the empty nest, having grandchildren, and then addressing the end of life (Carter & McGoldrick, 1988). Coming from this perspective, the tasks are less about biological, cognitive, or social development and more about adding and subtracting members from a system.

Many of our friendships are organized around developmental stages, as passing through developmental stages tends to be a particularly bonding experience. You can probably identify relationships in your own life that were created as you embarked on a new developmental stage. Further, much of our contemporary life is organized around developmental challenges. When I tell someone that my daughter is applying to college, it triggers a set of memories and beliefs about this stage of life. These memories and beliefs generally relate to both the physical tasks of the stage and the psychological tasks of the stage. If I am seeing friends whose children are also applying to college, it is almost impossible for us not to talk about all of the intricacies of the application process and then to circle back to the emotional anticipation of the upcoming transition. People generally use their own developmental experience as a reference point ("back in my day, we didn't do things this way"), so looking at developmental issues also triggers generational issues. It can be incredibly comforting to see that other people are struggling with the same challenges that one is currently facing, and it can be instructive to compare these struggles with those of previous generations. At the same time, an overemphasis on development can be alienating. Because I have an unusual medical condition, I can find it perplexing to hear my middle-aged friends talk about their aches and pains, knowing that my physical experience is out of sync developmentally.

THE PROBLEM WITH NORMALIZING

A true systems perspective will note the circular interplay between individual and systemic stages. Looking at individual and systemic development together allows us to understand and potentially normalize many of our clients' life tasks and challenges, without discounting the uniqueness of the individual situation. One classic example is looking at a couple with a new baby, and there is a fairly large body of research on the typical developmental challenges faced by a family at this stage (Gottman & Gottman, 2007). I remember getting a new case several years ago, as I was becoming acquainted with the family life cycle literature. The couple had a 15-month-old son, Aiden, and both partners were worried about the way they had grown apart since he was born. I felt that I did a fabulous job in asking questions about how their relationship changed when the baby was born. I looked at common themes of new parents being chronically tired and having little time for themselves or for each other. The wife, Jessica, talked about her physical exhaustion and the guilt she felt about no longer welcoming her husband's physical affection. The husband, Jack, discussed his increased anxiety about finances and his discomfort over feeling jealous of the attention Jessica gave to Aiden. I facilitated a discussion of these typical issues and normalized their stress and struggle.

At the end of the hour, they agreed to come back to therapy to work on increasing their connection during this stressful time. After they left, as I was walking down the hall, I was lucky enough to hear them in front of the elevator, around the corner. Jessica said, "That was okay, but I don't think she really understands us, and I'm not sure this is going to help." Jack responded, "Let's give her one more chance; maybe it will get better." I don't generally advocate eavesdropping, but in this instance I felt I had received a gift. I knew in the next session that I would need to pair my understanding of their life cycle issues with greater curiosity about their unique experiences as a couple.

USING DEVELOPMENTAL TRANSITIONS

So if simply describing and normalizing developmental issues may not be enough to help our clients, how is this knowledge of the life cycle helpful? In this example, I learned to go beyond a description of typical developmental challenges to look at the specific tasks of the cycle, the routines that need to be established to address these tasks, and the rituals that allow the system to come together and acknowledge the task. In this case, the tasks revolved around bonding with, caring for, and providing for the baby in a way that could enhance rather than undermine the connection between the couple. Typically, a new developmental stage will require new routines to meet the tasks of the stage, and in this case the couple described routines that weren't working for them. Jessica was surprised by how tired she was from caring for Aiden all day, and she was resentful of the long hours that Jack spent at his investment firm. Jack was stunned that Jessica would want him to take over the care of Aiden when he returned home in the evening, assuming that she would understand how tired he was at the end of the day. He would grudgingly give Aiden his bath, then Jessica would put Aiden to bed, and she would fall into bed shortly after. Jack would stay up and watch movies or surf the Internet.

Jack and Jessica brought me a similar fight about their Thanksgiving celebration, which took place at Jessica's parents' home. Jack had continued the tradition of organizing a football game with Jessica's brothers and father in the front yard of their home, while Jessica and her mother took charge of preparing the meal. Aiden became increasingly difficult to manage in the kitchen, and once Jessica reached the point of exploding, she went to ask Jack for help. Jack came in at the end of the game and took Aiden out of the kitchen, but by that point Jessica was furious with him. Jack felt betrayed by her anger, as he felt he was making a contribution to the family through the football game and by coming in to get Aiden, while Jessica felt abandoned and dismissed by Jack.

In both of these instances, I could have looked at the lack of communication between them and noted that the developmental task of caring for their toddler was going to require more negotiation. Using a life cycle lens to examine these routines and rituals added a depth to my understanding of the couple that set the stage for the communications work. Together, we explored the routines and rituals in Jack and Jessica's families of origin, and it became clear that their multigenerational models were contributing to their helplessness and frustration. Jack's father left the family when Jack was 4, and although the father provided for the family financially, he lived in another state and had only minimal contact with his children. Jack described his mother as mildly depressed, chronically overworked, but very dedicated to the family. Jessica reported that her father was passive, lacking ambition, but quite devoted to his family, and she experienced her mother as driven and ultimately frustrated. When we looked at expectations for daily routines, Jessica was proud of Jack's ambition but had a hard time understanding why he wasn't more eager to see Aiden at the end of the day. Jack's involvement with Aiden was so much greater than what he experienced in his own home that he could not relate to Jessica's disappointment. In contrast to his own mother, he had experienced Jessica as energetic and resourceful, and her exhaustion was perplexing to him. He would try to be helpful and a good sport, expecting appreciation from her, but instead she experienced him as distant and emotionally uninvolved, which increased her frustration.

We can see that when Jack and Jessica became parents, they each implicitly drew on models from their families of origin, unwittingly creating a distant, frustrated partnership that was deeply familiar but unsatisfying for both. As we looked at these family patterns, not only were we able to identify the disappointment that they each felt but also we began to craft a vision for a different kind of partnership. Jessica wanted Jack to be an ambitious provider and an involved father; Jack also wanted these things, but he didn't know how to do both. Similarly, Jack wanted Jessica to be a devoted mother and a romantic partner, and Jessica did not know how to do both. Jessica and Jack saw that Aiden's birth started them on the path of repeating family patterns but gave them the chance to create a relationship that was different from their parents' relationships.

Using the developmental tasks and context as a foundation, we were then able to explore new routines and rituals that would be more satisfying for both. For example, Jack was able to come home for dinner two nights a week so that the whole family could be together. On the nights that Jack worked late, he would bathe Aiden and put him to bed while Jessica went to the gym. Jessica found that she had more energy in the evening when she had spent time with Jack or had gone to the gym, so she stopped going to bed by herself, and the couple began spending time together most nights after Aiden went to bed. These changes show both a more successful adaptation to the developmental stage (meeting the physical needs of the baby and allowing both parents to bond with the baby and also maintaining their bond) and a reworking of family of origin themes for the next generation.

The life cycle perspective implies the existence of unconscious beliefs and expectations that are learned through our experiences with our families and other systems applications focus even more explicitly on unconscious determinants of our experience and behavior. You might not associate the study of unconscious forces with systems theory, and yet we have already seen that many of the pioneers of systems work in psychology, such as Bowen, Ackerman, and even Minuchin, had extensive psychoanalytic training (Nichols, 2010). Further, we have already noted that contemporary psychodynamic approaches borrow heavily from systems theory, to the point that intersubjective theory is described as a dyadic systems theory (Buirski, 2005).

EARLY TEMPLATES

It might be difficult to argue with the existence of unconscious processes because much of the information that we use day to day is processed outside our conscious awareness. A psychodynamic view of the unconscious moves beyond the idea that the unconscious is simply the culmination of perceptions that is not in our immediate awareness. Instead, the unconscious is the part of the mind that provides an unstated, deeply embedded view of self and others. The unconscious provides a template for making sense of relationships and is shaped by both innate and environmental factors. We might say that the unconscious is the repository for our felt experiences, the place where memories are organized into themes and issues. We can use the analogy of the computer operating system to understand the workings of the unconscious. I find this analogy helpful in that operating systems are comprised of instructions that are unseen to the computer user but are integral to the functioning of the program. As human beings, I believe that we all have unconscious operating instructions that help determine the way that we function with ourselves and function in the world.

REPARATION AND REPAIR

If we consider that the unconscious mind holds an organized schema that helps us filter and process experiences, it follows that the unconscious is a powerful force that is both mutable and resistant to change. Most psychodynamic theories agree that the unconscious is built through relational experience, but they differ in the extent to which they see developmental stage as crucial to the quality and type of intrapsychic structure that is built through interactions. Regardless of the emphasis on development, however, a view of unconscious templates for relationships helps us understand the idea of psychological repetition. In a very circular manner, our unconscious beliefs and expectations establish how we behave in the world, including influencing the type of relationships we seek. A more pessimistic view of this phenomenon, the repetition compulsion, highlights the Sisyphean aspects of human nature: We are often programmed to repeat rather than repair problems we have experienced in earlier relationships. This is especially true when conflicts remain unconscious and unexamined. A more optimistic view of this phenomenon highlights the ways that our unconscious templates challenge us to master previous conflicts and outgrow earlier relational problems. The traditional psychodynamic view takes the approach that by gaining insight, or making the unconscious conscious, we no longer need to act out the underlying conflicts. A systems view of these themes underscores the importance of insight but says that the work of the unconscious does not stop there. In addition, the resolution of unconscious conflicts allows us to then experience our relationships in new ways, which in turn allows us to behave differently in relationships.

If we look back at my dream, we can see the unconscious dilemma that is being triggered by watching my daughter's high school relationship. I believe that these challenges exist within me and within my daughter but are also passed down and across our family. In the second part of the chapter, we will talk more about the complementary patterns of intrapsychic defense, which is one fascinating application of a psychodynamic view to systems theory. But staying with a more individual approach, my dream suggests that her relationship has triggered some of my own ambivalence about individuality, growth, and loss. I am feeling guilty about leaving for college and having my own life, and I can feel good about this change only when I know that my boyfriend is settled in a new path. I awoke from the dream with a feeling of nostalgia and a bittersweet type of sadness, but it was not a particularly painful or confusing dream. Because I have explored these themes in depth, I not only have insight into these conflicts but also have applied the insights to alter the way I approach relationships. I am able to be more at peace with the breakup with my boyfriend in the dream, even though I was not able to be at peace with this decision when we were leaving for college. As I developed a deeper understanding of my conflicts about being autonomous and outgrowing the relationship, I could behave differently in the relationship, the relationship subsequently changed, and my view of myself was transformed. There was a circular process of intrapsychic and interpersonal work that facilitated greater mastery of these conflicts.

This view of the circular nature of internal and interpersonal themes is consistent with the work of object relations theorists, and many of these ideas have particular clinical utility (Scharff & Scharff, 1987). I especially appreciate the way that looking at deeper, unconscious determinants to behavior can add to our understanding of obstacles to change and opportunities for change. I can remember, early in my career, being amazed when couples stayed together in misery for decades, which doesn't appear to make sense from a strictly behavioral perspective. When a relationship makes us miserable, why wouldn't we try to get away from the misery, which is the very definition of negative reinforcement (the removal of a negative or punishing consequence)? Yet whether you label the phenomenon codependence or hostile dependence or give it some other label, both literature and popular culture are replete with examples of couples who seem to stay together to make each other miserable.

COMPLEMENTARY PATTERNS

One concept that has been especially helpful in understanding the maintenance and repetition of destructive patterns in relationships is projective identification. Melanie Klein (1946) does a brilliant job in describing this phenomenon, and I find Hannah Segal's (1973) explication of Klein's work to be very illuminating. Students are often put off by the more traditional psychoanalytic emphasis on the physical manifestations of early developmental phases, particularly more dramatic concepts like the good and bad breast. Yet the vivid and colorful theory adds to our understanding of human nature in at least two fundamental ways. First, anyone who has spent time with infants knows that the process of helping them learn to regulate their eating, sleeping, digesting, and alertness is a huge job that is often fraught with frustration. As we see throughout the chapter, the need for ritual, repetition, patience, and perseverance in meeting both individual and collective developmental stages is a huge contribution of dynamic theories.

The second major contribution of Klein's work lies in her thorough explication of projective identification. To understand the notion of projective identification, we need to quickly revisit Freud's definitions of defense mechanisms. According to Freud and other early psychoanalytic theorists, human beings develop defense mechanisms to cope with painful and difficult affective states, particularly those that relate to an overwhelming experience of anxiety. Even without a more thorough background in psychoanalytic thinking, most of you have probably heard of projection and its use as a defense. When we experience a particularly painful or negative thought or feeling, we can project it onto something in our environment, in essence, to get rid of it. Projective identification also starts with a negative internal experience, but one that is ambivalently held and integral to the definition of self. So instead of simply being able to get rid of the negative experience by projecting it onto someone else, the experience that is being projected involves a disavowed part of the self. Therefore, the ambivalence requires that the painful affect is both projected out and kept near. As we have already discussed with psychodynamic theories, the process of projecting something difficult and then identifying with the projection means that themes will be repeated, providing the opportunity of ultimately being mastered. In the case of projective identification, the mastery involves seeing someone else accept the projection and rework it in a way that it can finally be reclaimed and reintegrated into the self.

All of these psychodynamic descriptions may seem abstract and difficult to follow, but seeing this concept through a systemic lens also reminds us that projective identification takes place in real relationships, not in the netherworld of unconscious structures. Most psychodynamic systems theorists note that projective identification tends to involve a complementary process in which both members of a couple are projecting unwanted aspects of self onto the other (Catherall, 1992).

This interlocking pattern of dynamics can make miserable relationships hard to change, and it simultaneously makes systems work a powerful venue for change. It is certainly possible to experience projective identification in individual therapy, and much that is written about the constructive use of countertransference involves first accepting and then reworking projective identification from our patients. For example, Tansey and Burke (1995) do a brilliant job in describing the way that difficult countertransference reactions can be processed within the therapy in a manner that helps the client understand himself better and that allows for growth and repair of the therapy relationship.

REWORKING EARLY EXPERIENCE

Systems theory tells us that this countertransference experience is not only not limited to the therapy room but also can be foundational in creating and maintaining all kinds of intimate relationships. The case of Paul and Linda comes immediately to mind. They had been unhappily married for 22 years when they came to see me. They had been to couples therapy on two other occasions and almost proudly stated, "Communication skills don't work for us." They were currently embroiled in an enormous conflict around their 17-year-old daughter, Caitlyn, who was trying to decide whether to go to college. Linda felt strongly that Caitlyn should take a year off before going to college or try some kind of nontraditional program; Caitlyn's grades were poor, and she was not invested in searching for colleges herself. Linda believed that Paul had chronically favored and spoiled Caitlyn and that Paul would be willing to throw away the family's money on Caitlyn's college tuition, as he had always enjoyed throwing money away on Caitlyn. Paul believed that Caitlyn's problems stemmed from the high level of conflict between Linda and Caitlyn and that she would be fine once she left home. He believed Linda favored their son, Connor, who was a sophomore at an expensive college. He felt that it would be unconscionable to pay for Connor's education without doing exactly the same for Caitlyn, and he accused Linda of being unfair and punitive.

Although conflicts about paying for college are quite common in my experience, the feeling of being in the room with this couple indicated that there was more going on between them. Each partner had a high level of contempt for the other's position and seemed convinced of the other's negative motivation. In addition, their negative characterizations of the other were stable, comprehensive, well elaborated, and decades old. Linda described Paul as indulgent, selfish, and easily manipulated; Paul described Linda as ruthless, mean-spirited, and competitive. They could each find examples of seeing these characteristics in the other since early in their courtship. When asked the obvious question, "What keeps the two of you together?" each commented about asking themselves the same question, each agreed that it was important to provide stability to their children, and each quickly moved on to building a case against the other. Linda actively attacked Paul by pointing out all of his poor parenting decisions with Caitlyn; Paul's style was to let Linda's rage build and then comment on her toxic anger.

As their therapist, I knew that I needed to stop the destructive interaction between Paul and Linda, but I could understand why they said that in their previous therapy experiences, communication skills didn't work. Paul and Linda not only lacked the skills to employ a collaborative decision-making approach but also seemed unconsciously invested in resisting such an approach. As I got to know Linda better, I began to understand how betrayed and unimportant she felt in most of her relationships, including her early relationships with her parents. On the surface, she was a strong, bright, attractive, and accomplished woman who could hold her own in any situation. She expressed a great deal of contempt for Paul's passivity and struggled to feel any compassion for the way she hurt him when she attacked his character. I began to understand that she was projecting her experience of being small, vulnerable, and helpless on Paul in these moments. In their conflict, she behaved in ways that elicited feelings of inadequacy and incompetence, just as she had felt with her controlling, rejecting mother. At the same time, Paul's background set the stage for him to accept this projection and reciprocate. On the surface, he appeared friendly, easygoing, flexible, reasonable, and generous. In their interaction, it appeared that he was projecting his experience of being angry, frustrated, and indignant onto Linda. When we see each of these experiences as disavowed aspects of the self, we can have both the empathy necessary to connect with the emotionally charged experience and the commitment to reworking the projections so the pattern will change.

So how did Linda and Paul rework these projections? I do want to be clear that this type of intrapsychic work is notoriously slow and difficult, and most therapists would agree that a long-term history of chronically low satisfaction is not a good prognostic sign. But to reiterate the value of adding the intrapsychic approach, I have found that these theories help me form an empathic connection in challenging clinical situations, and coming from that position of realistic empathy, change is sometimes possible. In the case of Paul and Linda, the very slow and deliberate emphasis on turning their contempt into compassion gradually made the relationship more manageable. Further, because the issues they were trying to rework were so intertwined, the reclaiming of projections by one partner almost always resulted in the other partner's progress. When we worked on the legitimacy of Linda's anger and disappointment and helped her express these emotions more constructively, Paul gradually began to recognize and own his feelings of frustration and anger toward Caitlyn. Similarly, as Linda listened to Paul's struggle in supporting Caitlyn without being indulgent or becoming a martyr, she began to discuss her feelings of helplessness and vulnerability in wanting to be closer to Caitlyn.

This couple's work certainly included an emphasis on affect that is common in emotionally focused work but added a concentration on early experience. Paul recounted several memories of listening to his mother berate his father: He welled up with rage as he waited for his father to stand up for himself. His father quietly drank his way through these episodes, and the only time he did assert himself was when Paul tried to argue with his mother. His father then angrily insisted that arguing was disrespectful, and he punished Paul for speaking up. Initially, Linda saw Paul's discussion of his family of origin as an opportunity to gain ammunition against him; she stated that he had never looked at all of the pathology in his family. But as we connected the work on anger and vulnerability to current themes in their family and looked at how these themes related to both of them, Linda's growing compassion for her own internal experience allowed her to be more empathic towards Paul.

As you might imagine, the exploration of Linda's childhood memories mirrored what we worked on with Paul. Linda expressed a painful memory of having a high fever with the flu and needing to care for her younger sister, who was also sick, because her mother was too depressed to care for them, and her father was away. She was unsure about how to address her sister's misery, as she was only 7 years old and quite sick herself. Paul initially minimized Linda's description of her fear, joking that "since then Linda has been too tough to get sick." But concentrating on her feelings of being overwhelmed helped Paul accept his own fear, which in turn allowed him to be more affirming of her. When Linda was critical of Caitlyn for being immature, and when she tended to want to push Caitlyn out of the nest rather than nurture her, Linda began to understand that her extreme reactions made sense in the context of her family history. She became more open about her fear of Caitlyn's ability to care for herself, which Paul expressed openly, and as she owned this for herself, Paul held it less rigidly. They had started a circular dance in which each person's self-acceptance allowed greater acceptance of the other. Although progress was slow and certainly not linear, the work that Paul and Linda did on their relationship had enormous benefits for them as individuals and for their family. As they were more at peace with themselves, their communication improved, and they could actually employ some of the communication skills they had learned in their previous therapy. The task of the relationship became working together and enjoying each other, rather than their original unconscious contract of accepting the projections of the other.

The case of Paul and Linda shows a rather dramatic application of psychodynamic principles, yet this implies that psychodynamic theory is useful only when we need to understand psychopathology. In addition to understanding the importance of the unconscious, systemic psychodynamic theories highlight the relevance of individual and family development. In human systems, it is impossible to separate biological and social influences on development. Of course, a systemic view provides more than one way to look at phenomena, and the next chapter will challenge some of the universality ascribed to both family and individual developmental patterns.

Systems theory has utilized a multigenerational approach to development in two ways, incorporating both family life cycle perspectives and psychodynamic perspectives. The life cycle perspective highlights the importance of physical and psychological developmental tasks and looks at the routines and rituals that systems employ to navigate developmental transitions. A psychodynamic perspective emphasizes the unconscious relational template that is developed and then modified through intimate emotional interactions. Unresolved conflicts and needs are likely to be repeated in a complementary manner in subsequent relationships. This ongoing repetition both explains the prevalence of the multigenerational transmission of problems and illuminates the systemic opportunities to address problems intrapsychically and interpersonally.

CHAPTER 8

Social and Cultural Narratives

A BOUT 6 YEARS into our marriage, my husband and I had a fight that I consider to be a turning point in our relationship. As we were going to bed one night, he said, "So how long is it going to take you to get that sock into the hamper?" I earnestly replied, "What sock?" By now, we had been through numerous arguments about my poor housekeeping skills and about his tendency to be overly critical and demanding. But rather than having the same fight we had been through many times before, the lightbulb went on for both of us. As we processed what was happening, I learned that he was so frustrated with me that he had planted a sock on my side of the bed and was waiting to see how many times I would walk by the sock before I finally moved it. As you can tell from my response, I did not notice the sock in the three days that he was waiting for me to take action. The fact that he would go to the trouble to create this test for me stopped me in my tracks. Part of me felt that it was petty, but I realized that he must be in significantly more distress than I had previously acknowledged. If he was spending time thinking about how to finally get my attention, he must be more miserable than I had realized. Similarly, when he saw my reaction, he was clear that I was not being lazy or oppositional in resisting moving the sock. He finally saw that it was actually possible for me to walk by the sock without seeing it, something that he had not been willing to consider before.

As we talked through the problem in more depth, we ended with the kind of behavioral strategies that are discussed earlier in the book. I pledged to try to survey the room once a day and really pay attention to what needed to be put away; he promised to be more patient and gentler in talking to me about what was bothering him. We had tried this type of collaborative communication before, but somehow this

117

time was different. In the language of the last chapter, we now were able to approach each other with more empathy. But when I look back, I see that something happened that allowed the empathy to emerge. We each changed the way we defined the problem, because we created a new narrative about the problem. We began to say that we were fundamentally different in the ways that we notice and experience disorder and detail in our environment, with me finally believing that my husband needs order, cleanliness, and lack of clutter to feel calm and peaceful. My husband started to believe that I have a very thick filter for chaos and disorganization, so that I can tune out noise and clutter and still feel happy, calm, and grounded. We have told ourselves that these differences are innate and hardwired, so instead of trying to change each other, we are trying to work together in more effective ways.

Our new explanations of being physiologically programmed to approach household cleanliness differently allowed us to approach each other with greater acceptance, but are these explanations really true? We are able to find lots of evidence to support our belief in this explanation, looking at the sparse tidiness of his apartment and the piles of clutter in mine, the fact that he needs silence to work and I can have music blasting in the background, and so on. Of course, we knew about these differences from the beginning of the relationship, but after that fight, we modified the story of these differences in a way that made them easier to accept. As we reframed our differences as being out of our conscious control, our differences became something that we could laugh about and work on, rather than something we resented. Of course, we don't have any proof that these differences are hardwired, but that lack of proof didn't stand in our way in changing our perceptions of each other. Instead, when we told ourselves a different story about the behavior of the other, then we actually experienced that behavior differently.

THINKING MAKES IT SO

This knowledge that our experience is shaped by what we tell ourselves is not new. Shakespeare wrote Hamlet in 1599, and stated famously, "There is nothing either good or bad but thinking makes it so," (1992, p. 99) and moving on to more recent examples such as the *Power of Positive Thinking* (Peale, 1954), we know that human consciousness is built of an ongoing stream of self-talk that has the power to mold and modify our behavior. To look at the phenomenon more broadly, in the last several decades, the social sciences have been influenced by postmodernist philosophy, which looks at the way language shapes reality (Gergen, 2001, 2009). This line of inquiry challenges modernist ideas around truth, rationality, objectivity, and individual knowledge and encourages us to examine how socially constructed meanings can become accepted as objective truth. A common exercise to introduce students to the ideas of social construction is to hold up a $20 bill and ask students what it is. Literally, the bill is a piece of paper, yet as a society, we have agreed that the paper has a particular value. The agreement on the meaning of the $20 bill has ramifications for our daily experience, and while there is a predictable value for this currency in our culture, the actual value of $20 may be experienced differently, depending on the individual circumstances of the person holding the bill. Similarly, when I show students a small figurine of a woman in a white dress and a man in a tuxedo, they all know that it is a couple getting married, as this is a socially sanctioned symbol associated with marriage. Again, we see the ways that social meanings become reality and then can see the impact that these realities can have on social norms. Does this wedding symbol discourage two men from becoming partnered? Does it change a marriage if the participants can't afford a tuxedo rental? Is it meaningful to choose a different color wedding dress?

Regardless of your view of the ultimate nature of reality, you probably agree that our narratives influence our experience. If we acknowledge that narratives shape experience, then it follows that modifying narratives can also change experience. Within systems theory, recent developments in using narratives to promote change are worth exploring in more depth. Although the two schools of thought, narrative therapy and solution-focused therapy (Nichols, 2010), employ different techniques, they share a common emphasis on the power of language to shape our experience.

Narrative therapy was developed by Michael White and David Epston in the 1970s and 1980s and was influenced by social constructivism (White & Epston, 1990; White, 1995). This perspective, often labeled postmodernist, holds that rather than existing objectively, truth is consensually created through social discourse. Certain values, beliefs, and narratives may be privileged by the dominant culture, at the expense of other values, beliefs, and narratives that are silenced or marginalized. White and Epston noted that individuals create their own dominant narratives, influenced by their social networks, and it is often these dominant narratives that perpetuate both problems and suffering. For a variety of reasons, we are prone to create problem-saturated stories, which emphasize what is negative in our lives. In addition, certain social or cultural narratives may increase the chances that a person's dominant story involves self-blame or hopelessness.

LETTING THE PROBLEM BE THE PROBLEM

One major technique in narrative therapy is externalization, which sets the stage for reworking a problem-saturated story. Using the simple but elegant slogan "The person is not the problem; the problem is the problem," White and Epston (1990) highlight the importance of that problem definition. They note that when someone comes to therapy, he has often created a set of beliefs and worldviews that leave him feeling discouraged, flawed, and problematic. Within such a framework, the focus is on what is wrong with the person, rather than on the possibility for change. Using a variety of questioning techniques, White worked to help clients see their problems as separate from themselves and to help them develop a different kind of relationship with their problems. For example, Janey often came to therapy feeling exasperated by her inability to stop binge eating. She had a high level of self-loathing for this behavior, stating that she didn't know what was wrong with her and wishing that she could be different. As we discussed Janey's experience, we were able to talk about her binge eating as the problem, rather than labeling Janey as the problem. White sometimes went into elaborate detail in externalizing the problem, asking clients to give their problems names and describe them in ways that would make them more alive or real. Yet even without having clients formally externalize the problem in the manner suggested by White, I have found that the kind of questioning that places the problem outside the person is almost always helpful. To say, "When does binge eating get the best of you?" or "Do you ever feel that your binge eating persuades you to do things you really regret?" has a less blaming, more curious tone than most clients use with themselves.

A second technique that is common to narrative approaches involves exceptions to the problem story. Again, White and Epston were masterful in noting the ways that human beings can cling to negative, problem-saturated stories at their own expense. Similar to the concept of selective attention in cognitive theory, the idea of looking for exceptions assumes that clients selectively attend to problematic behavior that is consistent with the negative narrative, or problem-saturated story, and ignore aspects of experience that contradict this dominant narrative. With exception questions, the therapist draws attention to the times and conditions under which the problem was not influential, with the goal of helping the client illuminate a different aspect of the story. This positive emphasis both creates and further sets the stage for change. When working with my client who struggles with binge eating, I might say, "Tell me about the times you have been able to overcome binge eating this week" and "When did you find that binge eating wasn't able to present a challenge for you?" Again, the curious tone of these questions helps lay a foundation for changing the narrative and focuses attention on the positive as well as the negative.

In Janey's case, both the externalization questions and the exception questions helped her understand her relationship with her problem and notice when she was empowered to manage her problem more successfully. She observed patterns she had not noticed before, such as seeing that she was less likely to binge when she participated in a social event after work and that much of her bingeing seemed related to loneliness after work. Yet it is important to see that the insight about her loneliness was only part of the change that the narrative approach offered to Janey. In a more holistic way, she was able to shift both her behavior and her sense of herself when she made the shift from saying, "I am a binge eater" to "I am someone who overeats when I am lonely, and I need to find different ways to care for myself."

When I present some of these ideas to students, they often feel that the questions seem too formulaic, and they challenge the assumption that simply changing the story about a problem will actually change the problem. Often the issue isn't quite that simple, but I have found that the basic shift from defining the person as the problem to developing a greater awareness and understanding of the problems, separate from the self, often results in significant therapeutic movement. Whether we are talking about Janey's binge eating or my neglectful housekeeping, a narrative approach empowers the client to address the problem behaviors both realistically and creatively. The problem is simultaneously acknowledged as distressing and as something that needs to be addressed ("When does poor housekeeping cause problems in your marriage?") and seen as something that can be managed and approached directly ("When have you done a good job at overcoming poor housekeeping?"). The sense that part of the human condition is addressing problems over time and that we all have varying degrees of success in managing our problems is an inherent undercurrent in narrative approaches that represents a therapeutic shift for many clients.

THE CLIENT HAS THE ANSWER

In a similar manner, solution-focused therapy was developed in the 1980s by Steve de Shazer and Insoo Kim Berg (de Shazer, 1994). Again, although some of the underpinnings of the theory were different, the emphasis on using language and a constructivist philosophy to enhance change are quite similar. De Shazer and Berg built on the work of Milton Erickson and Jay Haley (Erickson & Haley, 1985) and the strategic therapists to create an extensive, deliberate emphasis on change. They felt that the mental health field emphasized psychopathology and problem etiology at the expense of focusing on strengthening the mechanics of change. De Shazer was famous for noting that you don't need to know how you got a flat tire to know how to change the tire. Of course, a true systems perspective would argue that there is value in knowing both how you got the flat tire and how to change the tire, and as a clinician, I think the idea of studying both problems and solutions is particularly important when problems tend to recur. But the solution-focused therapists were clearly in the forefront of contemporary psychology in highlighting the ways that psychologists have tended to focus on the negative and to know much less about solutions than we do about problems. This emphasis on looking at strength, resilience, and the innate human capacity for change is currently popular in the positive psychology movement (Seligman, 2002). Even before the positive psychology movement took hold, solution-focused therapists were operating from the perspective that human beings are hardwired to make progress and that it is the job of the therapist to maximize that potential for change.

Solution-focused therapy is known for a few specific techniques, and probably the best known is the miracle question. Generally, the miracle question is posed in the first session, and it is used both to establish goals for the treatment and to initiate the process of change. The instructions for the miracle question set up the following scenario for the client: "Imagine that tonight, while you are sleeping, a miracle occurred and the problem that brought you to therapy was suddenly solved. But because you were asleep, you didn't know that this miracle occurred. What would be your first clue that something had changed?" The therapist then goes on to explore all the ways that the client would know that the problem is indeed resolved. When there are multiple family members involved, all are asked to share their responses to the miracle question and to build on the others' answers. But the technique works equally well with individuals, with the same understanding that the therapist needs to have the ability to use the question to understand the client better and to set the stage for change. Janey first responded to the miracle question in a manner that is typical of many clients, by identifying a dramatic, fairy-tale solution that dodged the behavioral question. She started, "I would wake up 20 pounds lighter and would have a perfect body." We explored the ways that she wished a perfect body would provide her with a perfect life, but this inquiry quickly reached a dead end. When I asked what a perfect body would give her, Janey quickly went back to the psychological question at hand. She wanted to feel that she could accept herself and to be free of her preoccupation with self-improvement through self-deprivation.

Janey then went on to respond to the miracle question by talking about what wouldn't be happening, as she had a much harder time looking at what she actually wanted to have happen. She said, "I would wake up and I wouldn't worry about what I ate the day before and wouldn't start the day thinking about how I was going to starve myself today." This information about the way she feels trapped in a self-blaming cycle is useful, but the solution-focused approach does more than simply identify the negative, punitive self-blame. My challenge was to ask Janey what she would be doing instead that would really let her know that the problem was solved. As we discussed her wishes in more depth, she was able to talk about her desire to be more involved in what seemed truly meaningful to her, whether it was actually enjoying a beautiful morning or spending more time thinking about what she wanted to achieve at work. It was poignant to hear Janey finally take the time to imagine the morning when she knew the problem was solved; she would be able to notice how nice her shampoo smelled, listen to music on the radio rather than plan her diet, and write down items on her to-do list for work, so that she could think about her day on her way to work. Although each step was small, together they highlight a concrete vision of change that actually makes change more possible.

On the surface, the miracle question can appear to encourage a naïve positive attitude, trying to impose artificial happy endings for our clients to divert them from their misery. But effective use of the question reveals something different. One tenet of solution-focused approaches is that clients come to therapy with an implicit knowledge of their desired solutions, and part of the task of therapy is to make this knowledge explicit. By asking how the client would know that the problem was solved, there is an immediate shift to looking at direct, desired outcomes rather than at the absence of problems. In my experience, it is often both challenging and therapeutic to replace the language of problems with the language of desired solutions. As de Shazer's tire metaphor illustrates, describing problems and describing solutions are two separate and distinct tasks.

Another well-known technique in solution-focused therapy rates the severity of the problem as a means of starting the process of incremental change. The scaling question basically asks the client to rate the current severity of the identified problem and then identify specific ways to make the problem slightly better. Again, we might start by asking Janey, "On a scale of 1 to 10, with 10 representing no problems with eating, and 1 representing feeling totally miserable and out of control with your eating, how would you rate your binge eating this week?" Generally, whatever number is provided is greeted with a type of positive reframe: "Oh, a 2.5, that's not terrible!" But whatever number is given, the follow-up question is generally the same: "What would need to happen this week to raise your score by 0.5?" or some other very small amount. With both questions, the therapist works to reinforce the solution-focused premise, which is also the strategic premise—that systems inherently resist change, and it is the job of the therapist to establish effective conditions for a shift to occur.

Unlike the early strategic therapists, however, the solution-focused approach does not actively look for a paradoxical effect and instead banks on the ability of small, incremental alterations to begin a larger process of change. In this case, if Janey said that she rated her symptoms at a 4 this week, I would wonder with her just what it would take to move from 4 to 4.5. Here Janey responded that she would like to be able to go out to lunch with a coworker and order whatever she wanted, without worrying that her coworker would judge her and without second-guessing her choice later. As was true with the miracle question, the solution-focused approach allowed us to define specific behaviors that Janey wanted to try without being prescriptive or imposing the therapist's agenda. It was instructive to see that on some level Janey knew that she wanted to try to implement these modifications, but she had more practice in wishing for a superficial, easy cure and in being angry with herself that this cure had not occurred.

Of course, the difficult and counterproductive stories we tell ourselves don't occur in a vacuum, and both narrative and solution-focused approaches are explicit in identifying the social variables that can perpetuate problem-centered narratives. Part of what I especially appreciate about these approaches is the way they address the cultural context that shapes our core narratives. Rather than taking a simple approach to positive thinking and positive reframes, narrative perspectives in particular have examined the dominant narratives that create our realities. If I live in a culture that says women are intellectually inferior to men, for example, then the simple technique of challenging my cognitions around my intellectual inferiority is likely to miss the mark. Instead, a broader exploration of my understanding of my strengths and limitations as a woman and stories about the pain of these constraints would ultimately set the stage to rewrite some of these narratives in a way that provided more choices and greater empowerment. Changes in these dominant narratives often have impact at both group and individual levels.

REWRITING OLD THEMES

I like to tell the story of a time in graduate school when I challenged a dominant narrative and was fortunate enough to rewrite that narrative with one of my professors. This event occurred midway through my first semester of graduate school and started on the day that my class had turned in our first scholarly papers to one of our professors. Before class started but in front of the entire class, I told the professor that I had seen a review of his latest book in *Vogue* magazine, and I asked if he had seen the positive review. (He studied achievement motivation, and I suppose that the theme of the drive to achieve was relevant enough to be reviewed in *Vogue.*) He said he had not read the review and quickly began his lecture. The following week he returned our term papers and told us that our performance as scholars was highly disappointing. He talked about the need for us to develop more serious academic interests and spend more time in the library and less time reading nonacademic materials such as *Vogue* magazine.

As you can imagine, I felt humiliated in front of my classmates after my professor's lecture, especially because he had singled me out in mentioning *Vogue* magazine. But I was also angry when I thought about his comments, because I knew I had also spent a great deal of time in the library, and I had actually received a good grade on the paper he had returned. As I reflected on the sting I experienced from his comments and as I was feeling unfairly judged for reading *Vogue* magazine, I started to think that I needed to speak up to my professor about his potential sexism in equating *Vogue* magazine with low intellectual standards. I gathered the courage to march into his office to express my sense of being unjustly singled out, and luckily he was extremely responsive. He looked over my paper again and acknowledged that he hadn't made the connection that a *Vogue* reader could also have written a good paper. Further, he apologized to the class the following week for the comment and acknowledged that it probably did represent latent sexism that he was trying to address. As you can imagine, he gained a new measure of respect from me and from my classmates, and I felt empowered by the experience.

If we look at the incident from a narrative perspective, we see a conflict between two stories. My professor believes that reading fashion magazines is a sign of intellectual weakness and frivolity, and I believe that this view is sexist and erroneous. He is in a position of power and could certainly maintain that his view is correct; I could have accepted the dominant narrative and learned to hide my affinity for fashion magazines in order to be accepted in academic circles. Instead, something in the system allowed me to challenge this dominant narrative; certainly, part of what was helpful was the fact that he had written positive comments on my paper. If indeed the dominant story had been even more entrenched, he might have given all women in the class lower grades, which might have discouraged me from approaching him after class. But instead I was able to challenge his narrative, and we were both able to create a new story—for ourselves and for the group.

As is often true, I was struggling with two narratives, one stating that I could achieve and be successful and another stating that the conditions weren't right for me to succeed. Part of my struggle came from being a woman raised in the 1960s, at times directly influenced by sexism and at times supported by social change. When I chose to pursue the optimistic part of the narrative, believing that my professor's positive comments meant that he wanted to create an affirmatively nonsexist environment, I was taking a small, calculated risk that paid off for me and my classmates. Although I can never know the exact impact of this change, I do know that in the 20 years since our graduation, my female classmates and male classmates have been equally successful. How much is this success related to the fact that we have all co-created a narrative that takes the intellect of each gender seriously, regardless of their interest in fashion magazines?

I have seen clear benefits to applying a systemic understanding of the ways that humans narrate our experiences in my clinical work. One of the examples that I have seen repeatedly comes from the complex ways that our American culture shapes a couple's story of their sexual relationship. Often our narratives about gender and sexuality are implicit and invisible, but the lack of an explicit story makes these narratives no less powerful in shaping our experience. I'm reminded of the case of Tim and Gina, who had been married for 10 years when they came to see me in couples therapy. They were both earnest, thoughtful people who were determined not to hurt each other, yet they were perplexed by the distance between them and by the hurt that each felt. They were cordial and polite to one another, but both felt that their marriage had never achieved the warmth and closeness that they had hoped for when they were first together.

CHANGING GENDER NARRATIVES

One area of particular disappointment was their sexual relationship. Both described Tim as having a somewhat higher level of desire than Gina, but they described different ways that this discrepancy caused a problem. Gina said that Tim was prone to want to be close at inopportune times, and she was frustrated that he didn't put more effort into being romantic or courting her. Tim felt that Gina was looking for excuses to put him off and believed that the primary problem was her lack of interest. He was afraid that her desire was too low for them to have an adequate relationship, but he was equally afraid that she just wasn't attracted to him any longer.

One incident helped us examine the narratives that got Tim and Gina stuck in a pattern of avoiding their sexual relationship in a particularly painful way. On a warm summer evening, they had walked to dinner in their neighborhood and stopped in their front yard to pick flowers on the way home. Both described enjoying the evening and feeling more content than they had for some time. Gina was standing in front of the kitchen sink, putting water into a vase for the flowers, and Tim came up behind her, with one hand stroking her stomach and the other stroking her thigh. She angrily pulled away and asked, "Why did you do that?" He was bewildered by her response, saying, "I just thought that we could finally get together tonight." Each was extremely hurt by the response of the other, and they came to the session feeling hopeless and misunderstood.

The basic miscommunication in this example is striking. Tim is feeling close to Gina because they have had a nice evening together, and he is admiring the way she looks in her shorts. He touches her, wanting to be close, and has no idea that this will make her feel self-conscious and even objectified. When she becomes defensive, he doesn't understand what she is feeling. He expresses what he wants, but rather than this bringing them closer together, they feel further apart. At this point, they are operating from two entirely different cultural narratives, and I would argue that neither narrative is particularly helpful. When they examine what they both experience and believe, they have the chance to rewrite their sexual narrative in a way that can ultimately bring them together. By looking at their problem-saturated stories and the cultural contexts that create these stories, we can understand both the obstacles and the opportunities for change.

When Tim approaches Gina at the kitchen sink, he is admiring her and also desiring more physical closeness. He expresses this by touching her, and Gina experiences this touch as evidence of a dominant narrative: If you have a nice evening with a man, he will want to have sex with you. While there may be a kernel of truth to this story, you can see that when she narrates Tim's approach in this manner, she is doomed for disappointment. This story is about men wanting sex, not about Tim wanting to be close and affectionate with her. In addition, he approaches her in a way that makes her feel self-conscious. She is worried about the size of her stomach and thighs and feels self-judgment rather than pleasure when he touches her. Tim feels Gina tensing up when he touches her and does in fact judge her, not for the size of her stomach and thighs, but for her reluctance to relax and be close to him. He starts on his own narrative: Women like sex only at the beginning of a relationship, or pretend to like sex until they get a commitment, therefore he feels hopeless that Gina will have interest in being sexual with him. Again, there is a kernel of truth in his narrative, but it misses several key components. He has no understanding that Gina may need to work on becoming more comfortable with her body to be more appreciative of Tim's sexual advances.

Like the sock story that started the chapter, we can see clear behavioral changes that would allow this couple to function better. If Tim was better at using words to express his appreciation for his time with Gina, and if he began his physical affection with kissing and other activities that were less loaded for Gina, she might believe that his sexual desire could bring him closer to her rather than that he simply wanted to use her for a sexual release. In a parallel manner, if Gina was more accepting of her body and more direct in expressing her own sexual desires, Tim would feel less rejected and more empowered to create a satisfying relationship for both of them. The cultural context around gender is central in creating the misunderstandings that are evident in this story, and creating a new story about their sexual desire is essential to establishing and maintaining their behavioral change.

Even more specifically, what I liked about working with Tim and Gina is that the gender-based themes in their sexual conflicts are common to so many couples that I see and are so helpful to change. Although Tim was resentful of Gina's lack of desire, he was also ambivalent about his own desire. "As a man" he was not upset with himself for having desire, but he didn't know much about how to talk about his desire, and he was very easily shut down when Gina was not in the mood. Luckily, he was civil and respectful enough to know not to push the issue, but because he didn't want to be forceful, he backed away from his own desire very easily. When I said to him, "I think it is a wonderful thing that you still want your wife," he looked at me with astonishment. It was clear that he felt that his desire was an annoyance, although he believed that he couldn't help having these inconvenient feelings. At the same time, it was helpful to see that Gina's experience of her own sexuality was rooted in ambivalent gender messages as well. When Gina was younger, she felt thin enough and attractive enough to believe that she warranted Tim's attention, but over time she stopped connecting his desire to an appreciation for her. She experienced their sexual relationship as something that existed for him rather than for them, and she didn't have the model or the language to explore the ways that could make those aspects of the relationship better for her. Instead, she had a vague fantasy that if he was "more romantic," then she could feel more sexual.

In this case, both narrative and solution-focused techniques were very helpful in setting the stage for change. When we worked on the miracle question, it was fascinating to see both Tim and Gina identify similar themes in their wishes for warmth and affection. They talked about their desire to make eye contact in the morning and to snuggle in bed at the beginning and end of the day. Both realized that they had been avoiding each other in this way, feeling hurt and also punishing each other. When we looked at exceptions to the pattern, both could remember times of feeling special and appreciated sexually, but both were shy about having a direct conversation about these memories.

A discussion of their mutual desire for connection provided a foundation for them to develop new themes in their sexual relationship. Tim was able to talk with her about feeling alive and aroused in a way that Gina hadn't heard before. Both were able to expand a previous understanding of "Tim is a man, so he wants sex" into something that was more positive and more relational than it had been before. Gina was able to replace the story "Gina is a woman and wants to avoid sex" with an understanding of wanting to feel special and desirable in a way that was less about being good enough or about being objectified and more about being able to give and receive pleasure with less self-consciousness. I'm focusing on just one set of themes here, and the reality of this case was less linear than I am implying. But it was useful for me to see that the change in these narratives allowed them to approach both self and other with more curiosity and less judgment and that ultimately these changes allowed them to treat each other differently.

Contemporary systems theorists have embraced the postmodernist emphasis on the importance of language in shaping experience. Building on the idea that reality is socially constructed, systems approaches have looked at the ways that dominant narratives can perpetuate individual and social problems. By recognizing and confronting the problem-saturated stories that inhibit change, narrative therapists challenge clients to separate the person from the problem and empower the person to develop a different relationship with the problem. Similarly, solution-focused therapists help clients identify their own solutions and then use positive language to set the stage for incremental change. Each of these approaches reinforces the importance of context and the circular nature of change.

CHAPTER 9

Applications to Theory, Research, and Organizations

C OMING FULL CIRCLE from where we started, I continue to believe that systems theory is an invaluable lens through which to examine human behavior. I've tried to illustrate the ways that systemic concepts have enriched my work with individuals, couples, and families. The beauty and the frustration of systems theory is that it can be applied so broadly, and in my experience, the value of systems theory is not limited to the therapy room. I have also found that systemic concepts are extremely valuable in understanding and integrating psychological theory, in evaluating and improving psychological research, and in participating in and managing groups and organizations. A full description of these applications of systems theory is clearly beyond the scope of this book, but I can't resist ending by challenging you to continue to utilize a systems perspective in all of these ways.

As you can see from the various family therapy theories that I have drawn from throughout the text, systems theory can easily be used as a metatheory, which can serve as a foundation for the other major psychological schools of thought. Systems theory works best on broad, big-picture patterns or on specific, moment-to-moment interactions, and I often find it helpful to fill in an intermediate level of analysis with other psychological theories. A both-and approach to psychological theories would indicate that it is naïve to try to see which theoretical tradition is correct or holds the ultimate truth. Instead, our knowledge of context and the importance of perspective allow us to ask more sophisticated and helpful questions: What are the strengths and limitations of the theory? How is the theory similar to other theories, and what are the key differences? What is gained and what is lost by combining the theory with other theories? For me, a useful metaphor in looking at psychological theories is seeing them as distinct languages. Like languages, many psychological theories share common foundations yet, through regional and historical developments, have evolved into distinct entities. Using this metaphor, I would argue that systems theory can serve as a metatheory, just as there is a broad theory of human speech and language acquisition that transcends any separate language. As psychologists, there are probably more advantages to being theoretically bilingual than monolingual, but what is even more important is to recognize and respect the fact that each theory speaks its own language. My experience is that a background in systems theory provides the broad perspective that allows us to know that all languages are in fact human speech and also provides a common platform to create better understanding between different theories.

SYSTEMS THEORY AS PLATFORM

In addition to creating respectful dialogue between theories, systems theory can serve as an organizing structure to integrate theories. While several promising integrative models have been developed (Breunlin, Schwartz, & Kune-Karrer, 1992; Gurman, 2008), I have the greatest familiarity with Pinsof's integrative problem-centered therapy model (Pinsof, 1994), and here I'll briefly present the ways that this model both rests on and is infused with core systemic principles. Pinsof's model is not a theory; instead, it provides an organized way to utilize major psychological theories. It is designed to be cost-effective, to maximize treatment outcome by allowing therapy to be individualized, and to capitalize on a wide repertoire of intervention strategies.

Pinsof has updated his model to include additional factors (1995), but for brevity I have taken the liberty of presenting in Figure 9.1 an older model (Pinsof, 1994), which includes slightly fewer variables. The themes and application of the model are similar in both versions, as I have found that both offer conceptual clarity and therapeutic utility.

Pinsof first organizes three therapeutic modalities, left to right: family therapy, couples therapy, and individual therapy. Along the left side of the grid, Pinsof highlights three types of psychological theory: behavioral theories, experiential theories, and historical theories. As it is drawn on the grid, you can see that it is possible to do individual, couple, or family therapy from a behavioral, experiential, or

Modalities/Contexts

	Family/Community	Couple/Dyadic	Individual

Orientations

Behavioral/Interactional
— Social learning
— Strategic
— Functional
— Structural

Experiential
— Cognitive
— Affective
— Communication
— Interpersonal

Historical
— Family of Origin
— Psychodynamic
— Psychoanalytic

Figure 9.1   Pinsof's 1994 Integrative Problem-Centered Orientation/Modality Matrix

historical perspective. Frequently, clinicians see clients in all of these modalities, and whether they actually work with a case in all of these formats or work collaboratively with another therapist; clinicians are accustomed to thinking about the way that a problem is organized at each of these levels. Similarly, most clinicians have at least been exposed to each of these types of theory, and most psychotherapy research suggests that clinicians choose to pull from more than one theoretical tradition in working with clients, whether they label themselves as eclectic or integrative in orientation. Further, we could argue that most contemporary theories are inherently integrative, regardless of whether they use that label. The cognitive-behavioral theories bridge two levels of Pinsof's model, and current psychodynamic theories combine the experiential and historical levels.

Regardless of the semantics of describing each model, I find that the levels that Pinsof describes are distinct enough to clarify my thinking and help me organize the intervention strategies that I will use. The behavioral level looks at concrete, observable behavior and focuses on

the importance of direct behavioral change. Specific theoretical traditions listed at this level include behavioral couple and family therapy,
strategic therapy, and structural therapy. The overt goal at this level is
for clients to experiment with new behaviors and to treat each other
differently. In contrast, the experiential level looks at the felt and
thought experience of the clients in the room. This immediate, here-
and-now experience is the focus of intervention. The goal is to raise
consciousness about the ways that thoughts and feelings contribute to
problems. Ultimately, thoughts and feelings should either help to solve
problems or help to enhance relationships. Theoretical traditions that
are grouped in this level include the work of Virginia Satir (1972) and
Carl Whitaker (1977), but this level also includes emotionally focused
and cognitive approaches. The third level of the model is dedicated to
historical approaches, which examine the role of the unconscious in
determining both behavior and experience. This level incorporates both
psychodynamic and family-of-origin perspectives. The common thread
at this level is the way that earlier experience creates templates and
patterns that are then pursued and repeated.

There is no single way to apply the model, and I consider the model
to be a map that helps me describe and plan my options for intervention in the room. Pinsof states that to be most cost-effective, it is best
to start treatment in the left top area of the grid and then move to
smaller groups of people and more involved theoretical strategies as
needed. All things being equal, it is assumed that working on direct
behaviors with the most people possible in the room will allow the
most expedient results. However, Pinsof points out that the overarching principle in the treatment is the therapeutic alliance, and the
creation of a positive alliance requires collaboration with the client.
Part of establishing the treatment relationship is hearing the client's
understanding of the problem and utilizing the client's preferred way
to address the problem. The therapist may choose to work in a sequen-
tial way with the client, proceeding through each level as needed, or
may choose interventions from a variety of levels in each session. The
style and flow of the sessions will emerge as the therapist guides the
client through the possible treatment options, finding the best match
for the client's needs.

We see that this model combines a wide variety of family therapy
theories, but how does this model actually use systems theory? We can
answer this question on a couple of levels, first looking at the theories
themselves and then looking at the client. In looking at the ways that the
theories are combined, we see the influence of multiple perspectives

and the clear foundation of multiple and circular causality. Although the grid is drawn in a linear manner to fit the two-dimensional space, in reality we see that the theories are organized in a circular fashion with bidirectional influence. Each theory exists in relation to other theories, sharing the ability to be applied in different modalities but having unique contributions to our understanding of the problem. Finally, the model rests on a systemic understanding of change, with the assumption that change is both sought and resisted. Understanding that problems are maintained in multiple ways and at multiple levels, we see that there are numerous choices for change when it becomes impossible in the form that we initially chose.

When we look at the systemic elements of the work with the client, first and foremost, the model is based on relationships. The therapist works to establish a warm, caring relationship that recognizes the many contexts in which the client is embedded. The therapist acknowledges circular and multiple causality by helping the client move from blaming someone for the problem to empowering the client to act for change. In sum, the model rests on the both-and perspective, acknowledges the role of context, takes a balanced and creative perspective on change, and emphasizes collaborative communication between the therapist and client and between clients.

The case of Tim and Gina in the last chapter provides a rich example of the benefits of using a systemic, integrative therapy. Tim and Gina were a motivated, likable couple who were invested in therapy, but their progress was slower and more uneven than any of us would have hoped. They were initially referred for couples therapy by Tim's individual therapist, who had worked with Tim on his long-standing depression. As Tim's individual functioning had improved, he noticed problems in the marriage that he wanted to address. At the beginning of therapy, Tim and Gina noted that they had always loved traveling together, but they had curtailed much of their travel 3 years ago, when they purchased a new home. Tim felt that Gina was constantly scheduling home projects for him to do and was critical and demanding in the way she managed these projects. Gina felt that Tim resisted doing his fair share in their new home and believed that she carried too much responsibility for their household. We initially worked on communication skills, helping them hear each other's concerns and make more direct requests of the other. We identified their pattern of bickering followed by avoidance and helped them replace it with a clearer negotiation of time and tasks. Both were relieved to be able to address their concerns more overtly, and the behavioral emphasis allowed them to feel less negative in the relationship. But both reported that something was still missing, and the therapy felt flat and uninspired.

Although their initial complaints were improved, none of us felt that the therapy had achieved its goal, and I was grateful to draw on the systemic integrative model I have described to understand what still needed to change. I began to explore their complaints on an experiential level. Tim talked about all that he felt he had lost during the time he was depressed. He was grateful to Gina for her patience and steadfastness, but once he felt better, he didn't know how to recapture a feeling of vitality and connection with her. He tried to prove his devotion by stepping up his participation around the home, but instead of feeling admired and acknowledged by Gina, he felt unappreciated. Gina also explored her feelings of having to be strong and steady when Tim's functioning had decreased. She was pleased that he was feeling better but realized that she was still waiting for him to acknowledge the full extent of her efforts during his difficult time. During this stage of exploring their emotional distance, the incident at the kitchen sink described in Chapter 8 occurred. At this point, we explored their thoughts and feelings in much greater depth and also helped them make sense of their experience in the context of their gender beliefs and expectations. They were warmer and more understanding of one another but again felt that something was holding them back from experiencing the kind of comfort and excitement they had felt earlier in their marriage.

Similar to the stage I described earlier, rather than seeing the lack of satisfaction as a problem, we were all able to sit with the sense of dissatisfaction and wonder what still needed to change. Tim was able to express the guilt he felt for burdening Gina with his depression and came to understand that he had similar guilt around his sexual desire for her. But sharing these feelings did not help Tim move through them, and we began to explore some of the earlier roots of these feelings of guilt. We went through a similar process with Gina, in that she got stuck in feeling that there was no room for her to have wants or wishes in the marriage and then was completely unable to articulate what those wants and wishes were. As we moved forward in the therapy, Tim was able to talk about his father's poor treatment of his mother and the guilt he felt in not doing more to protect her from his father's abusive temper. His ambivalence about "being a man" was made even more complex by the negative feelings he continued to harbor toward his father. In contrast, Gina's father had died when she was an adolescent, and she had immensely positive memories of him. She felt that she was the one in the family who kept it all together when he died and that she had never had the chance to fall apart and have someone else care for her.

In this case, the combination of the behavioral, experiential, and historical levels of intervention were all used to help Tim and Gina rekindle their feelings for one another, which in turn reenergized their marriage. We worked on their dynamics as a couple and on each of their individual issues. Although each of these approaches was helpful separately, the real power of the intervention came when the approaches were combined. Tim and Gina were able to understand their issues in the context of their current communication, their cultural context, and the patterns they internalized through their developmental and family experiences. Without a systems perspective, they might have pursued behavioral change or might have achieved insight into the family patterns that they were repeating, but the systems perspective allowed them to consolidate these changes in a way that helped each feel strongly supported and deeply understood. They left therapy feeling they had a clearer knowledge of themselves and each other and that their capacity to love each other and to feel loved was what they had hoped for early in their marriage.

MAXIMIZING THE UTILITY OF RESEARCH

I have made the case that systems perspectives can help us understand, evaluate, and work with psychological theories, and I believe that the same concept can be applied to psychological research. In Chapters 2 and 3, we looked at many of the limitations of traditional Western research, in particular at the danger of applying a reductionist, isolationist lens to the study of any human phenomenon. To take this critique a step further, systems theory offers a rich template through which we can also understand, evaluate, and work with psychological research. On a very basic level, we understand that research can be misused to support almost any argument and that the conclusions of much psychological research are impossible to correctly interpret. I'm afraid that I am infamous in my family for quoting psychological research to my advantage. I can think of a recent example of a study I saw in passing that stated that men who are close to their mothers make better romantic partners. I didn't look up any of the details of the study before I mentioned it casually at dinner to bolster my belief that the close relationship I share with my 15-year-old son benefits him as much as it benefits me. By now, my family teases me about any comment that begins with "The research shows," but this example helps me see the ways that systems theory actually helps me become a dramatically better producer and consumer of research. In this instance, I saw the research conclusion ("Sons who are close to their mothers are better partners"), and yet I know very little about how this conclusion was drawn and what it really means. I am using the research in a clearly inappropriate way—justification for staying very close to my son, because this will help him be a better romantic partner later in life. I am adding a second piece of research evidence to my conclusion, which is that people who are better romantic partners have a higher quality of life. ("The research says. . . . ") From a commonsense standpoint, I can argue that both of these contentions make sense. But are they really supported by research?

A systems perspective will say that research doesn't confirm or disconfirm truth but instead helps us clarify questions and our assumptions so that we can answer our questions in a manner that is consistent with our assumptions. In this instance, I am assuming that the researcher has defined closeness to mother and being a good romantic partner the same way that I would define these variables. I don't know anything about the sample used to draw these conclusions or whether the sample really makes the case I want to make. Is the study based on 60-year-old men who are still close to their 90-year-old mothers? I certainly aspire to be close to my son when I am 90, but I am curious whether I could generalize the results of this study to my relationship with my 15-year-old son. Moving beyond the context of the sample that was used in the study, we need to look at the specific ways the concept is defined or the language used to communicate the question and the results. Would I still agree with the conclusion of the study if they defined closeness to mother as sleeping in the same bed as mother? In my house, this would not work. Yet in other cultures, this might be a perfectly reasonable definition of closeness to mother. Finally, systems theory will ask us to go beyond the issues of context of population and explicit definition of constructs to the problem of causality. In this instance, I am using the research to state that being close to one's mother causes a good romantic relationship later in life. In fact, it is highly plausible that a good romantic relationship helps a man stay close to his mother (something that would also be fine in my future, by the way).

If we are looking to ask better questions and understand the extent to which research can answer questions, then systems theory has much to offer. In this instance, I tracked down the original research. In a study done on 33 dating college couples, there was a positive correlation between men reporting that they were close to their mothers and happy with their partners (Roberts & Stein, 2003). Intuitively, we might say that men who have learned to be close to women through their close relationships with their mothers will apply this learning in their young adult relationships. I have no problem entertaining this idea and hope the researcher takes her initial finding and tries to explore this further. But we should be clear that this correlation means only that in a small sample, college men who reported being close to their mothers also reported being happy with their partners. Without investigating more about the study, we don't know whether being close to one's mother was also correlated with liking macaroni and cheese, being good at tennis, and being polite to strangers (all things that are true for my son, at least!). We also don't know whether these same men who report being close to their mothers will report being close to their professors, their dogs, and their mailmen. Are the correlations spurious? Did the men who reported being close to their mothers also report being close to everyone else? The fact that correlation gets linked to causality and that ultimate truth is erroneously gleaned from methodological artifacts, is well documented in the research literature.

My example may be far-fetched, yet we can see in many examples from the hard sciences that research can be misleading and that research that is done to isolate phenomena can be particularly misguided, as life in the real world does not involve isolating phenomena. Liking macaroni and cheese may actually be more predictive of having a satisfied partner than the other variables I mentioned. But if this is so, why would it be true? Are macaroni-and-cheese eaters happier with all aspects of life? Do people who are partnered with macaroni-and-cheese lovers treat them better because they are easier to please? Systems theory shows us that these questions aren't easy to answer but that it is important to ask the hard questions. Further, systems theory helps us see that critical thinking, ultimately, is contextual thinking.

As a clinician, I also find that a systemic perspective allows me to utilize research in a realistic and helpful way with my clients. One of the most replicated findings in all of couples' research is the outcome that it takes five positive interactions to counteract the effects of one negative interaction (Gottman & Gottman, 2008). I find this research fascinating, as it confirms my clinical experience that negative interactions are more powerful than positive interactions. Yet I certainly would not advocate keeping a tally of positive to negative interactions. How do I know that this research is valid, and how can I use it as a clinician? To begin with, I do believe that clinicians have the responsibility to read and utilize research and have much to learn from our research colleagues. When I look at the studies that track the positive to negative ratios, I can see that the researchers are diligent in pursuing a meaningful question and are also willing to admit evidence that disconfirms their hypotheses. In this instance, it was initially believed that negative interactions were toxic and that the most important element of couples therapy was stopping negative interactions. Yet a more careful study showed that couples could have a high level of negative interactions as long as the positive interactions were high enough to adequately balance them. How does this apply clinically?

In addition to helping us adequately address issues of context and causality, systems theory challenges us to develop solid communication that allows a respectful, consensual perspective on reality. With clients, this focus on collaborative communication creates a win–win situation when it comes to reporting and using research, and I hope that this perspective ultimately adds to our ability to evaluate and revise research. In the therapy room, I have learned to say, "The research states that this pattern is common. Is this pattern true for you?" I have found that knowing and mentioning the research not only adds to my credibility but also speeds up the process of understanding a problem, whether the clients agree with my research perspective or not. When I say, "The research indicated that it takes five positive interactions to counteract the effects of one negative interaction. Is that true for the two of you?" I find that the question is meaningful, whether they agree or disagree. If a client says, "Yes, that is so helpful! I feel so guilty after I jab my partner, but if I remember that I can say five nice things afterwards, I know I can make it better," then I believe that the research has been put to good use. On the other hand, when a client says, "That statistic doesn't mean much to me, because all negative comments are not created equal. Some might take 2 positive comments to undo, and some might take 10," then as the clinician I can keep the discussion going to better understand the types of repair that will work with various types of jabs. Again, a systemic perspective on research would not suggest that research gives us the truth, just a single perspective on truth, which can always be revised.

Given current concerns about the need for scientific evidence for the efficacy of psychotherapy, I think a systems perspective is more necessary than ever before. A systems perspective can help us be clear and realistic about what we know, so that we not only say, "Cognitive behavioral treatments have been shown to be effective in treating anxiety" but also say, "Cognitive behavioral treatments have been studied more frequently than any other treatment for anxiety. When cognitive behavioral treatments are compared with other treatments, they tend to fare better than other treatments a small percentage of the time and then fare as well as other treatments the rest of the time. Psychodynamic treatments tend to fare better when clients have chosen them directly and don't fare as well with random assignment." Again, this type of subtle, gray-area analysis is not easy to do and not popular in a winner-takes-all type of competition for superior treatment, whether the prize is status or insurance dollars. But systems theory offers the opportunity to look at that gray-area alternative to the one-size-fits-all approach.

The newer research question, "What treatments are most effective, under what specific conditions, for which specific patients?" is a classic systems question. And the ability to apply research findings in a circular, recursive manner completes the systemic approach to research. If I am able to bring the research findings to my clients, they can say which part of the research is relevant and how they would change the parts that are not relevant. Over time, a systems perspective would suggest gathering these data from my clients and feeding it back into the research in some way. I might tell a researcher, "Your findings suggest that a 5–1 ratio of positive to negative interactions is important, but this average seems to miss something important clinically. Repeatedly, I have heard that there is a qualitative difference between the types of negative interactions that truly need repair. Could you please do some additional research to give me more insight into the difference between negative interactions that need repair and those that don't?" In the win–win paradigm of good systems work, the researcher would thank me for my helpful insights, and I would thank the researcher for her useful conclusions. We would see that in this complementary process, our experiences created a stronger perception of reality together, similar to the teacher's advice to the blind men with the elephant. Although it may appear that I am being somewhat simplistic in laying out this opportunity for collaboration, I earnestly believe that a true systemic collaboration is needed to move forward both the art and the science of psychology.

ORGANIZATIONAL EFFICACY

A final way to apply systems theory outside the therapy room occurs in the day-to-day work of our organizations, and it is easy to approach that work systemically, even without taking on political agendas. As I look at my own behavior in organizations, I see that systems theory has helped me prevent problems and maximize success, even when I was unaware that I was using systems theory. When I was doing my postdoctoral fellowship, I was asked by my supervisor to set up a family therapy consultation service at a community agency. Looking back, I am immensely grateful for my systems theory training, because I can see that without this training I would have probably made several key mistakes.

As I was setting up the program, I spoke with my supervisor about its goals. We established a detailed outline of the services that I should provide, which centered on using my family therapy expertise to strengthen the skills of the staff in the community agency. But his final response was "Above all else, keep the agency happy," and this seemingly insignificant remark both shaped the program and fostered my relationship with the staff. I went into the program expecting that I was going to sit in meetings and develop trainings for the paraprofessionals who dealt directly with the pregnant and parenting teens in the community program. But based on the words of my supervisor, I spent most of my initial energy trying to develop a working relationship with the staff, and of course, utilizing my knowledge that it is generally good practice to start a new process by joining with the target system.

As I observed the implicit communication that was taking place about the families who were discussed in our meeting, I correctly clarified that the community center wanted me to provide direct service to the families, in spite of this being a different vision than what had been provided at my agency. But I was able to be clear in my desire to create a service that would meet the needs of the community center, and my ability to develop and communicate a collaborative plan was important in establishing the success of the program, as I would see over time.

My next challenge was facing the issue of confidentiality. I had wondered why the agency had been so reluctant to send family therapy cases to the community mental health center down the street, and I quickly learned at least one of the obstacles. The community support staff openly shared information on every client and felt that mental health personnel withheld crucial information that would have helped the clients. The expectations of the staff were that I would report on what happened in the sessions so that they could use this information in working with their clients. In contrast, I expected that my sessions would be entirely confidential unless I needed to take emergency action around a safety issue. As I thought about what was communicated by keeping confidentiality and what was communicated by sharing infor- mation, I was able to see both sides more clearly. I knew that I needed to fit in with the norms of their system enough to be accepted, and yet I wanted to be a distinct entity and to provide a service that was not already available in the system. I saw the classic need to be a differen- tiated member of the system, with a separate identity and the ability to be connected to the system. To achieve this differentiation, I had to practice clear, affiliative communication. As I started each treatment, I let the clients know that I met with the staff on a weekly basis and that we all liked to work together, so that clients often found it useful for me to share information with the staff. At the same time, therapy was an endeavor that worked best when clients felt their concerns were held privately, which reduced the need to plan and censor communication. Given these competing demands, I structured the sessions so that at the end of each session, we would determine just what information I should share with the staff. Then, at the beginning of the next session, I could review any information from the staff meeting with the clients.

At first, I felt that this very deliberate and explicit emphasis on boundaries and communication was more for me than for the clients, but they seemed to indulge me in the regimented way that I began and ended each session. As time moved on, however, I found that my emphasis on clear communication actually established the kinds of rules and boundaries that made my role different from that of other staff members. My clients knew that they could talk about whatever they wanted during the session but that we would end a session with a plan on how this information would interface with the larger system. At times, the sessions yielded little information that needed to be shared; at other times, sharing information was crucial. I came to see that my distinct role and the clear expectations for the functions of my role were both essential elements in the success of the program. The functions of my role were to help my client feel empathically supported (which was protected by the confidentiality) and to feel empowered with additional problem-solving resources (which was enabled by the planning we did at the end of each session and my work with the rest of the staff). Both of these functions were made clear in my communication and therefore were evident in the structure of the therapy system that was established.

Although there were other challenges to establishing the family therapy program, another issue arose a year into the program that was especially enlightening for me. After providing family therapy services for a year, I was invited to do a parenting workshop for the staff. This workshop was exactly the type of task I had envisioned performing when I first went to work at the center, and I was very excited about working with the staff in this way. I prepared numerous worksheets and clinical examples, and I brought in my favorite parenting books to show the staff. I was talking about the importance of rules and consequences, and I had passed around the parenting books for the staff to examine. One of the staff members stopped me midsentence to say, "This book says it isn't okay to spank your kids." Not understanding the implicit message in his communication, I responded, "Exactly! The book that you are looking at outlines the parenting philosophy that I have been using here with our clients, and emphasizes the importance of using discipline methods other than spanking." Initially, I had expected that the staff would be relieved to have this philosophy described in such a clear and distinct manner, but the incredulous looks I was receiving from the staff helped me understand that that there was more going on with this topic.

I knew that I needed to sit back and hear the perspective of my colleagues, and I could see that many of them were passionate about their perspective. They felt that they had been told that spanking was wrong, yet many had experienced spanking as a key act of parenting that showed them that their caregivers were involved and had high standards for them. I began to understand a bit about the cultural context of spanking and saw that what I considered to being angry and out of control was instead interpreted as signaling engaged concern. Luckily, the staff had worked with me long enough to see that I had helped families have discipline, order, and structure; although they hadn't realized that I had supported these goals without corporal punishment. At the same time, I saw that these staff members were the success stories of the neighborhood and that I couldn't discount their belief in spanking without further thought.

At the end of the workshop, we agreed to disagree. The staff understood that I had been asking clients not to spank their children and had instead been working with them to find other effective means of discipline and behavioral control. The staff also saw that I had not needed to make a single child abuse report (although I had helped them make a neglect report, based on the experience of a family they were seeing), which helped them understand that my mission was not to punish the behavior of those in their community, but to improve functioning. I came to feel that the staff was impressed to know that I had achieved such good results without recommending spanking, although of course I didn't achieve these results, the families in treatment did. But the whole dialogue opened our eyes and helped us confront some of the preconceived notions we all held about managing behavior and about each other. Ultimately, I was not willing to change my stance on spanking and continued to feel that multiple parenting techniques were more humane and more effective. But I changed my knee-jerk reactions to spanking and learned the importance of constructive dialogue, both in hearing a very different perspective and in asking that my perspective be heard. I learned a great deal about the importance of cultural context and of multiple means to the same end.

FULL CIRCLE

As I have mentioned, I believe my systemic training in creating healthy boundaries, using good communication to solve problems, and allowing multiple viewpoints was essential to my success in the neighborhood family therapy program, and I continue to use these principles in many areas of my life. I certainly don't believe that systems theory is the only approach that has utility value, and I worry about coming across as ending this book with a sales job. But I need to be forthright about my reasons for writing this book, which occur at a couple of different levels. On an intellectual level, I find systems theory a satisfying and reliable home base through which to consider the challenges of the day. Whether I am reading Michael Pollan's discussion about food policies in our country (which I find fascinating), or whether I am looking at the relative merits of public and private schools, I find that going back to the basic tenets of systems theory helps organize and elevate my thinking and broadens my options for constructive behavior. I have the same experience of clarity and efficacy when I use systems theory with my clients. When I know enough to evaluate the basic systems questions, I find that I am well equipped to move forward with the problem at hand. Although a specific question list might be endless, I like to organize my thinking around the following seven questions:

1. What are the various *contexts* in which the problem is embedded? How would I describe the problem or issues in terms of biological, individual, couple, family, or community levels of involvement? How do these systems and subsystems work together, and how do they compete?

2. How does each member of the system describe the *cause* of the problem, and how can this causality be reframed? What is the circular pattern that maintains the problem, and what are the multiple factors that reinforce this pattern?
3. What is being *communicated* about the issues at hand? What are the conflicts between the explicit and implicit communication about the problem? How could the communication work better and be more effective?
4. What are the forces that encourage the issue to *change*, and what are the forces that resist change?
5. What are the rules, roles, and boundaries that establish the *structure* of the most relevant system? How is the structure functioning well, and how does the structure contribute to the problem?
6. What are the *historical and developmental* patterns that are being repeated in the system? How do these patterns cause resistance to change, and how do these patterns provide identity?
7. What are the *cultural stories* that influence the problem? How do these invisible stories reinforce oppression and inhibit empowerment? How can these stories be used for greater self-acceptance or to promote change?

Both in my work as a therapist and in my work as a professor, I have had the privilege of addressing these kinds of questions. I have witnessed the way that within healthy relationships, systems theory can promote flexibility, clarity, and curiosity. Armed with those three powerful allies, the work of creating healing and stimulating relationships is truly inspiring. I hope you find the same inspiration in this work.

References

Ackerman, N. (1966). *Treating the troubled family*. Northdale, NJ: Jason Aronson.

Anderson, C. M. (1986). *Schizophrenia and the family: A practitioner's guide to psychoeducation and management*. New York, NY: Guilford Press.

Anderson, V. A. (1997). *Systems thinking basics: From concepts to causal loops*. Waltham, MA: Pegasus Communications.

Bandura, A. (1977). *Social learning theory*. Englewood Cliffs, NJ: Prentice-Hall.

Bateson, G. (1972). *Steps to an ecology of mind*. New York, NY: Ballantine Books.

Bateson, G. (1979). *Mind and nature*. New York, NY: Dutton.

Beebe, B., & Lachmann, F. M. (2002). *Infant research and adult treatment: Co-constructing interactions*. Hillsdale, NJ: Analytic Press.

Bertalanffy, L. v. (1968). *General system theory: Foundations, development, applications*. New York, NY: Braziller.

Bowen, M. (1985). *Family therapy in clinical practice*. New York, NY: Jason Aronson.

Breunlin, D. C., Schwartz, R. C., & Kune-Karrer, B. M. (1992). *Metaframeworks: Transcending the models of family therapy*. San Francisco, CA: Jossey-Bass.

Bronfenbrenner, U. (1979). *The ecology of human development*. Boston, MA: Harvard University Press.

Buirski, P. (2005). *Practicing intersubjectively*. Lanham, MD: Jason Aronson.

Buirski, P., & Haglund, P. (2001). *Making sense together: The intersubjective approach to psychotherapy*. Northvale, NJ: Jason Aronson.

Carter, E. A., & McGoldrick, M. (1988). *The changing family life cycle: A framework for family therapy*. New York, NY: Gardner Press.

Catherall, D. (1992). Working with projective identification in couples. *Family Process*, 31(4), 355–367.

Christensen, A., & Jacobson, N. S. (2000). *Reconcilable differences*. New York, NY: Guilford Press.

Davidson, M. (1983). *Uncommon sense: The life and thought of Ludwig von Bertalanffy (1901–1972), father of general systems theory*. Los Angeles, CA: J. P. Tarcher.

De Shazer, S. (1994). *Words were originally magic*. New York, NY: W. W. Norton.

Erickson, M. H., & Haley, J. (1985). *Conversations with Milton H. Erickson, M.D.* New York, NY: Triangle Press.

Faloon, I., Leff, J., Lopez-Ibor, J. J., May, M., & Okaska, A. (2005). Research on family interventions for mental disorders: Programs and perspectives. In N. Sartorius (Ed.), *Families and mental disorders* (pp. 235–257). New York, NY: John Wiley and Sons.

Fisher, R. & Ury, W. (1991). *Getting to yes: Negotiating agreement without giving in.* New York, NY: Penguin Books.

Fraser, J., & Solovey, A. D. (2007). *Second order change in psychotherapy: The golden thread that unifies effective treatments.* Washington, DC: American Psychological Association.

Freud, S. (1909). Analysis of a phobia in a five-year-old boy. In S. Freud, *Collected papers* (Vol. III). New York, NY: Basic Books.

Freud, S., & Strachey, J. (1962). *The ego and the id.* New York, NY: W. W. Norton.

Gergen, K. (2001). Psychological science in a postmodern context. *American Psychologist, 56*(10), 3–32.

Gergen, K. (2009). *An invitation to social construction.* Washington, DC: Sage.

Goldner, V. (1985). Feminism and family therapy. *Family Process, 24*(1), 31–47.

Goldner, V., Penn, P., Sheinberg, M., & Walker, G. (1990). Love and violence: Gender paradoxes in volatile attachments. *Family Process, 29*(4), 343–364.

Gottman, J. M., & Gottman, J. S. (2007). *And baby makes three.* New York: Crown.

Gottman, J. M., & Gottman, J. S. (2008). Gottman method couple therapy. In A. S. Gurman (Ed.), *Clinical handbook of couple therapy* (pp. 138–164). New York, NY: Guilford Press.

Greenberg, L. S. (2002). *Emotion-focused therapy: Coaching clients to work through their feelings.* Washington, DC: American Psychological Association.

Gurman, A. S. (2008). Integrative couple therapy: a depth-behavioral approach. A.S. Gurman, Ed. *Clinical handbook of couple therapy.* New York, NY: Guilford Press.

Haines, S. G. (1998). *The manager's pocket guide to systems thinking & learning.* Amherst, MA: HRD Press.

Haley, J. (1963). *Strategies of psychotherapy.* New York, NY: Grune & Stratton.

Haley, J. (1973). *Uncommon therapy: The psychiatric techniques of Milton H. Erickson, M.D.* New York, NY: W. W. Norton.

Haley, J. (1976). *Problem-solving therapy.* San Francisco, CA: Jossey-Bass.

Haley, J. (1980). *Leaving home: The therapy of disturbed young people.* New York, NY: McGraw-Hill.

Hanson, B. G. (1995). *General systems theory beginning with wholes.* Washington, DC: Taylor & Francis.

Hayes, S., Follette, V., & Linehan, M. (2004). *Mindfulness and acceptance: Expanding the cognitive-behavioral tradition.* New York, NY: Guilford Press.

Hayes, S., Strosahl, K., & Wilson, K. (1999). *Acceptance and commitment therapy: An experiential approach to behavior change.* New York, NY: Guilford Press.

Heims, S. J. (1991). *The cybernetics group.* Cambridge, MA: MIT Press.

Hoffman, L. (1981). *Foundations of family therapy: A conceptual framework for systems change*. New York, NY: Basic Books.

Jacobson, M., & Christensen, A. (1998). *Acceptance and change in couple therapy: A therapist's guide to transforming relationships*. New York, NY: W. W. Norton.

Jacobson, N., & Margolin, G. (1979). *Marital therapy: Strategies based on social learning and behavioral exchange principles*. New York, NY: Brunner/Mazel.

Johnson, S. M. (2002). *Emotionally focused couple therapy with trauma survivors: Strengthening attachment bonds*. New York, NY: Guilford Press.

Johnson, S.M. (2004). The practice of emotionally focused couple therapy. (2nd ed). New York: Brunner/Routledge.

Karson, M. (2008). *Deadly therapy: Lessons in liveliness from theater and performance theory*. Lanham, MD: Jason Aronson.

Karson, M. (2010). Personal communication

Kerr, M. E., & Bowen, M. (1988). *Family evaluation: An approach based on Bowen theory*. New York, NY: W. W. Norton.

King, D. B., & Wertheimer, M. (2005). *Max Wertheimer & Gestalt theory*. New Brunswick, NJ: Transaction.

Klein, M. (1946). Notes on some schizoid mechanisms. *International Journal of Psycho-Analysis, 27*, 99–110.

Koestler, A. (1979). *Janus: A summing up*. New York, NY: Vintage Books.

Kuhn, T. S. (1970). *The structure of scientific revolutions* (2nd ed.). Chicago, IL: University of Chicago Press.

Laszlo, E. (1972). *Introduction to systems philosophy*. New York, NY: Gordon and Breach.

Linehan, M. (1993). *Cognitive-behavioral treatment of borderline personality disorder*. New York, NY: Guilford Press.

Markman, H. J. (1993). Preventing marital distress through communication and conflict management training: A four and five year follow-up. *Journal of Consulting and Clinical Psychology, 61*(1): 70–77.

Markman, H. J., Stanley, S., & Blumberg, S. (1994). *Fighting for your marriage: Positive steps for preventing divorce and preserving a lasting love*. San Francisco, CA: Jossey-Bass.

McIntosh, P. (1988). *White privilege and male privilege: A personal account of coming to see correspondences through work in women's studies*. Wellesley, MA: Wellesley College, Center for Research on Women.

Minuchin, S. (1974). *Families and family therapy*. Cambridge, MA: Harvard University Press.

Minuchin, S. (1997). Structural family therapy. In *Seeds of hope: Harvesting the heritage of family therapy in Chicago*. Chicago: University of Illinois at Chicago.

Minuchin, S., & Fishman, H. C. (1981). *Family therapy techniques*. Cambridge, MA: Harvard University Press.

Munger, M. P. (2003). *The history of psychology: Fundamental questions*. New York, NY: Oxford University Press.

Napier, A., & Whitaker, C. A. (1978). *The family crucible*. New York, NY: Harper & Row.

Nichols, M. P. (2010). *Family therapy: Concepts and methods*. (9th ed.) Boston, MA: Allyn and Bacon.

Nichols, M. P., & Schwartz, R. C. (2001). *Family therapy: Concepts and methods* (5th ed.). Boston: Allyn and Bacon.

Patterson, G. R. (1970). Reciprocity and coercion: Two facets of social systems. In C. A. Neuringer (Ed.), *Behavior modification in clinical psychology*. New York, NY: Appleton-Century-Crofts.

Patterson, G. R. (1971). *Families: Applications of social learning to family life*. Champaign, IL: Research Press.

Patterson, G. S. (1993). Outcomes and methodological issues relating to treatment of anti-social children. In T. Giles (Ed.), *Effective psychotherapy: A handbook of comparative research*. New York, NY: Plenum Press.

Peale, N. (1954). *The power of positive thinking*. New York: Prentice-Hall.

Pinsof, W. (1994). An overview of integrative problem centered therapy: A synthesis of family and individual psychotherapies. *Journal of Family Therapy, 16*(1), 103–120.

Pinsof, W. (1995). *Integrataive problem-centered therapy: A synthesis of family, individual, and biological therapies*. New York: Basic Books.

Pittman, F. S. (1987). *Turning points: Treating families in transition and crisis*. New York, NY: W. W. Norton.

Pittman, F. S. (1989). *Private lies: Infidelity and the betrayal of intimacy*. New York, NY: W. W. Norton.

Pollan, M. (2006). *The omnivore's dilemma: A natural history of four meals*. New York, NY: Penguin Press.

Pollan, M. (2008). *In defense of food: An eater's manifesto*. New York, NY: Penguin Press.

Rampage, C. (2002). Working with gender in couple therapy. In A. A. Gurman (Ed.), *Clinical handbook of couple therapy* (pp. 533–545). New York, NY: Guilford Press.

Roberts, S., & Stein. S. (2003). Mama's boy or lady's man? *The Variance of Psychological Science: Within and Between*. Atlanta, GA: American Psychological Society, 15th Annual Conference.

Satir, V. (1972). *Peoplemaking*. Palo Alto, CA: Science and Behavior Books.

Satir, V. M. (1983). *Satir step by step: A guide to creating change in families*. Palo Alto, CA: Science and Behavior Books.

Scharff, D., & Scharff, J. (1987). *Object relations family therapy*. New York, NY: Jason Aronson.

Segal, H. (1973). *Introduction to the work of Melanie Klein*. New York, NY: Basic Books.

Seligman, M. (2002). Positive psychology, positive prevention, and positive therapy. In C. Snyder (Ed.), *Handbook of positive psychology* (pp. 3–9). New York, NY: Oxford University Press.

Senge, P. (1990). *The fifth discipline: The art and practice of the learning organization.* New York, NY: Doubleday.

Shakespeare, W. (1992). The tragedy of Hamlet, prince of Denmark. (Barbara Mowat and Paul Werstine, eds). New York: Washington Square Press.

Sheehy, N. (2004). *Fifty key thinkers in psychology. Routledge key guides.* London: Routledge.

Siegel, D. J., & Hartzell, M. (2003). *Parenting from the inside out: How a deeper self-understanding can help you raise children who thrive.* New York, NY: J. P. Tarcher/Putnam.

Skinner, B. (1974). *About behaviorism.* New York, NY: Knopf.

Solovy, A. D., & Duncan, B. L. (1992). Ethics and strategic therapy: A proposed ethical direction. *Journal of Marital and Family Therapy, 18*(1), 53–61.

Tannen, D. (2001). *You just don't understand.* New York, NY: Harper.

Tansey, M. A., & Burke, W. F. (1995). *Understanding countertransference: From projective identification to empathy.* New York, NY: Routledge.

Wachtel, E. F., & Wachtel, P. L. (1986). *Family dynamics in individual psychotherapy: A guide to clinical strategies.* New York, NY: Guilford Press.

Walters, M., Carter, B., Papp, P., & Silverstein, O. (1988). *The invisible web: Gender patterns in family relationships.* New York, NY: Guilford Press.

Watzlawick, P., Bavelas, J. B., & Jackson, D. D. (1967). *Pragmatics of human communication: A study of interactional patterns, pathologies, and paradoxes.* New York, NY: W. W. Norton.

Watzlawick, P., Weakland, J. H., & Fisch, R. (1974). *Change: Principles of problem formation and problem resolution.* New York, NY: W. W. Norton.

Weinberg, G. (2001). *An introduction to general systems thinking.* New York, NY: Dorset House.

Wertheimer, M. (1959). *Productive thinking.* New York, NY: Harper.

Weisstein, Eric W. (2010) "Young Girl-Old Woman Illusion." From *Math-World*—A Wolfram Web Resource. http://mathworld.wolfram.com/YoungGirl-OldWomanIllusion.html (accessed June 28, 2010).

Whitaker, C. (1976). The hindrance of theory in clinical work. In P. J. Guerin (Ed.), *Family therapy: Theory and practice.* New York, NY: Gardner Press.

Whitaker, C. A. (1977). *The family crucible: The intense experience of family therapy.* New York, NY: Harper Collins.

Whitaker, C. A. (1981). Symbolic-experiential family therapy. In A. A. Gurlman (Ed.), *Handbook of family therapy.* New York, NY: Brunner/Mazel.

White, M. (1995). *Re-authoring lives: Interviews & essays.* Adelaide, Australia: Dulwich Centre Publications.

White, M., & Epston, D. (1990). *Narrative means to therapeutic ends.* New York, NY: W. W. Norton.

Wiener, N. (1948). *Cybernetics: Or control and communication in the animal and the machine.* [Cambridge, MA]: Technology Press.

Author Index

Subject Index

Lightning Source UK Ltd.
Milton Keynes UK
UKOW01f1301160915

258715UK00001B/12/P